Deird

SOS
For survivors of suicide

Reprint: Originale edizione: giugno 2007

© 2005 - 2014 Deirdre
McNamara

All rights reserved. All reproduction prohibited without authorisation of Author and Publishers. Tutti i diritti riservati. Riproduzioni anche parziali sotto qualsiasi forma sono vietate senza autorizazzione dell'Editore e Autore.

INDEX

ORIGIN   p 3

CHAPTER ONE
Historical and Contemporary Attitudes to Suicide   p 9

CHAPTER TWO
Social and Political suicide   p 17

CHAPTER THREE
Social factors in Ireland's high suicide rate   p 25

CHAPTER FOUR
Seniors and Suicide   p 29

CHAPTER FIVE
Endogenous depression   p 33

CHAPTER SIX
Depression -endogenous and extrinsic   p 37

CHAPTER SEVEN
Early childhood factors   p 41

CHAPTER EIGHT
Addiction/Alcoholism   p 45

CHAPTER NINE
Prescription Drugs and suicide   p 53

CHAPTER TEN
Paraholism   p 63

CHAPTER ELEVEN
Domestic Violence   p 69

CHAPTER TWELVE
Adolescence   p 77

CHAPTER THIRTEEN
Homosexuality p 91

CHAPTER FOURTEEN
Age related factors p101
Economic factors p107

CHAPTER FIFTEEN
Physical disease and depression p111

CHAPTER SIXTEEN
Traumatic Brain Injury p115

CHAPTER SEVENTEEN
Post Abortion Syndrome p 119

CHAPTER EIGHTEEN
Post Natal Depression p125

CHAPTER NINETEEN
Strategies for Survival p129

CHAPTER TWENTY
Masks and Mirrors p133

CHAPTER TWENTY ONE
After bereavement p137

CHAPTER TWENTY TWO
Coping with the ultimate tragedy p141

CHAPTER TWENTY THREE
More on strategies p145

CHAPTER TWENTY FOUR
Postlude p149

ORIGIN

Foreword

"On Suicide" is written as a response to a letter received after one of my articles was published in "Irish Catholic."

The writer said that she had tried to obtain information on suicide and help for survivors; that very little was available and that the editors whom she had contacted avoided the subject like a plague, apart from the occasional announcement that Ireland was the leader in suicides of young males.

I have counseled persons experiencing suicidal ideation, and persons who survived or witnessed suicides. It's too easy to plant labels such as "narcissism, selfishness, rage-filled." These may or may not factor in, but the lasting sensibility in the suicide victim is intolerable pain.

Tragically, it is a pain they pass on to their shocked survivors.

Depression may appear to lift prior to the act. "He seemed to be doing better..." is the cry of the bewildered survivors. The "recovery" is in fact the decision to relinquish the struggle. The boundary into fantasy has been crossed.

"SOS - (For) Survivors of Suicide" is not intended as an academic text.[1] Some topics merit a book or five of their own. I have tried to give a comprehensive overview of a very painful subject in the hope of providing consolation and insight to persons suffering from the knowledge that their beloved spouse, child, sibling, cousin, friend, acquaintance, boss, teacher, neighbour, died by his/her own hand.

I've personally experienced the "what if" - what if I'd called the suicide person when I came across their business card a month prior to their suicide.

---

[1] The Merck Manual provides fact based-information on treatment options and protocols for suicidal patients. As a homeopathist I respect the seriousness with which suicide is regarded there; I do however, find the underlying ethos somewhat harsh.

What if I had complimented them on their work in a certain field? Would it have "made a difference?"

If a person is in so much pain that they end their lives violently, traumatically, in freedom, the decision and responsibility is his or hers alone.

Tragic though it may be, Free Will is the God given right of each individual, for which each individual is accountable.

Though we cannot undo the act and return our loved one to life we can find healing and emotional protection in the company of peers; in a support program or with the support of a private counselor or therapist. The loss will never go away, but the pain becomes bearable over time.

IN CRISIS OR EMERGENCY.....

Friend,

If you are experiencing suicidal ideations; if your emotional pain level is approaching unbearable, then put down this book and take one of the following actions:

- **Call** a trusted counsellor,* member of the clergy, Samaritans or other hotline.
- **Abandon** the pain zone. If you are alone in your room, dress comfortably and leave immediately.
- **Go** to hospital, church, your doctor or a Twelfth Step Meeting even if you do not belong to that group. Sit and listen.
- **Do not remain alone and unconnected.**
- Open the book of psalms. Read them aloud.
- Sit by the Blessed Sacrament until the moment passes.

The atmosphere of prayer and silence permeating Christian places of worship are open to all persons of peace.

Check for HALT [1]

Are you Hungry? Eat a good meal.

Are you Angry? Breathe slowly, then find the origin of your anger and ask if it is worth your life.

Are you Lonely? You may not be able to reverse a bereavement, undo a family estrangement or romantic disaster but you can find comfort in group activities.

Twelve Step groups often have open meetings. There is no requirement to speak or identify yourself. They thrive on anonymity. Walk in, pour yourself a coffee or water and absorb the grace.

Are you Tired? Then rest! The exhausted mind cannot defend itself.

If you are "obsessing" and cannot rest, "change the tapes/dvd." Go to a movie, rent uplifting, soothing or humorous dvds, listen to music, dive into a gentle book, concentrate on a neglected task.

Where depression is a reaction to external factors, eg, loss of job or romance, sharing with a loving friend or family member is usually preferable to the "institutional route." However, as friends and family are not legally bound by confidentiality, a level of maturity and responsibility is essential. If there's any doubt about the ability of your friend or family member to keep a secret or cope with the confidence, then consult a *professional, ASAP*.

Where ideations are persistent or prolonged, always seek professional help.

Whenever possible, avoid medications. They eventually wear off often leaving the patient feeling worse, and must be used under strict supervision. Some psychotropes require escalating doses and, despite extensive lab testing, only reveal their quirks and idiosyncrasies when utilised by a broader population.

[2] Alcoholics Anonymous for persons unable to tolerate, process or limit alcohol.

Patients may withhold symptoms, side effects, prescription abreactions [3] or deterioration in their condition in order to "please" their physicians. A dedicated doctor prefers to know if you are experiencing side effects so that he/she can modify the prescription to your individual needs. If medication is necessary make sure your doctor is sensitive to individuality of each prescription. Remember the physician has a duty of care to you, not the reverse; you are not required to protect him or her. Respect, yes! Protect - no!

Most doctors have an authentic [4] "calling" to relieve human suffering. Their instinct and desire is to help their patients. They would prefer to know when a "tablet" isn't helping to seeing a patient institutionalized or buried, so speak up. It's good therapy for you, and might not only save your life but improve its quality.

There is only one of you in the world.

You may never know how your presence affects the people around you.

Get a complete physical. Many chronic illnesses are masked by depression. For the homeopathist and acupuncturist, depression is a symptom of underlying pathology, not a "disease" in itself. The patient must be free, wherever possible, to make his/her choice of treatment. If physical disease is "hiding" under the smokescreen of depression, the sooner the discovery, the more rapid the recovery.

Rent and watch "It's a Wonderful Life" to its conclusion.

HELP LINES, IRELAND

Numbers may change or vary according to locality, so they are not included here. Helplines are listed in the phone book or available via the Eircom operator.

There are many more support groups and help lines in Ireland that are excellent by repute. The following have been particularly recommended.

---

[3] *Atypical or unusual reactions indicating need for prescription change*
[4] *The degree of empathy can vary. Find a doctor who genuinely cares for your wellbeing and relates well to you.*

Post Suicide - Console,
Suicidal thoughts and impulses - Samaritans
Crisis pregnancy - Curam (Crisis pregnancy)
Domestic Violence hotlines

A sympathetic pastor is a great blessing. Some pastors are more gifted in administration than in soul guidance. Seek out a pastor who is kind and emotionally honest. If you fail to establish a rapport, keep searching until you find the support that you need. It's out there.

If winter come can spring be far behind? (Shelley)
It's always darkest before the dawn...

8

CHAPTER I

HISTORICAL AND CONTEMPORARY ATTITUDES TO SUICIDE

In 1792, Dr. Samuel Hahnemann, the genius who developed the Homeopathic system of cure, was the first doctor to include suicidal impulses as a biophysical symptom.

Up to then, attitudes to suicide were mired in superstition. It was considered a diabolical act and suicides were denied Christian burials. Silence was the expected response; the bereaved were expected to hang their heads in shame, bottle their grief and visit the gravesites after dark.

As psychiatry developed, strongly influenced by Hahnemann's work, enlightened practitioners of orthodox medicine started to treat suicide as an illness, *mental* illness.

Priviliged populations, usually patients in higher income brackets, received psychotherapy; the poor were given pills to suppress their symptoms. With psychotropes come the risk of the rebound effect and lifelong dependency.

Homeopathist continued to treat suicides quietly and successfully, earning many converts, as with the physician that saw the effect of one dose of one remedy in the case of a woman determined to take her life *by any means available*.

There were no suicides during Dr. Joseph Cooper's tenure as psychiatrist at Westchester Co Jail during the fifties and sixties. There were suicides before and after. Cooper was an MD Homeopathist.

Contemporary attitudes to suicide have matured, and the body may be buried in consecrated ground. Specialised counselling is available to the bereaved.

The prevailing attitude to suicide is that the act is one of anger, repressed, internalised rage.

The etiology of suicide is diverse. Addiction; unresolved grief; guilt; shame; depression; hopelessness; sudden loss of home/business/employment; debt; bereavement; somatopsychosis - mental illness rooted in physical disease, such as hormonal/endocrinal malfunction.

In the matriphobic eighties it became fashionable to "blame mother". The cult of the bad mother became imprinted on our minds as Hollywood turned from "I Remember Mama" to "Don't throw Mother from the Train" and other such horrors.

These were part of a strategy to damage the image of mothers, and implant mistrust in the minds of impressionable adolescents, in order to clear the way for the destruction of the Euro Christian family and the creation of baby as commodity, embryo as medical "spare bits" and the continuing horrors spewed out of government, ie, taxpayer funded laboratories. It succeeded. An entire generation of Americans misinterpreted maternal guidance as "control," and since unprecedented numbers were raised without Dads in residence, or a significant number of predatory step Dads. [5]

Consequently, naïve American teenagers were being plucked off the street, lured into communes, exploited by "gurus," murdered by drug lords, etc., ad nauseum.

Who benefits? Drug lords for one. Our response: build more prisons...

The approach of a new century or millennium tends to bring out and reveal the angst and attitudes of the previous era. In the last decades of the second Millennium the Hemlock Society emerged, politically correct and determined to encourage as many white Euro-Christians as possible to terminate their lives. They issue carefully worded instructional pamphlets on methods that make it impossible for a suicide to call for help or stop midway, should he/she change his/her mind.

As with abortion, the secular humanists kick in with media support - plays, movies, articles on "death with dignity". It worked with abortion. Almost 50 million Americans *of various ages* are missing and will never come back.

[5] *(this does not refer to men of character who raise step children with love and generosity as bonafide stepfathers)*

Chapter I

They were destroyed *in utero*. Now, the generation that fought so aggressively for "womens' rights" is the first to face mass euthanasia. It's going on already. Just not officially. Back to Hemlock's version of the "right to destroy oneself."

Imagine a poor woman, paralyzed by drugs, hearing a mother's voice on the phone machine, or the boyfriend who had rejected her apologizing and saying let's make a go of it.

Hemlock has her sitting in a bathtub, drugged to the gills, unable to climb out and pick up the phone. They don't tell her that she may change her mind but will be too paralysed to do anything about it.

Or a man, out of work to the point where he believes he's unemployable, bullied by debt collectors, unable to respond to a job offer that comes in as he takes his final breath. Hemlock's response would probably be something glib like "turn off the answering machine."

Hemlock's methods disable and disempower the human person, and mock the term "dignity."

There is no dignity in their methods.

There is no dignity in a bunch of cops and paramedics looking at your bloated naked body.

There is no dignity in being hauled out of a bath-tub, placed in a body bag and dragged out of a house or building.

There is no dignity in the autopsy process where the body is sliced open, organs removed, weighed and tested for substances, etc., before being returned to a shocked, grieving and angry family.

I will not specify techniques recommended by organizations promoting self-inflicted violence as some readers may be vulnerable to suggestion.

The motivational strategy is the underlying fear of an ageing Baby Boomer population unable to care for themselves and becoming dependent on public support. Ironically, the population that bullied the legislature into legalizing "nice, safe" abortion is now bombarded with articles "romanticizing" "death by choice" as there is insufficient youth to care for them. The injustice of coerced wholesale abortion has come around, but subsequent generations are left with these values as a starting point. Almost fifty *million American citizens* have been surgically dismembered *in utero* since Roe vs. Wade. [6]

Today's youth are savvy, and determined to avoid the traps and pitfalls of the pothead generation. Mass Media in the eighties seemed directed toward the destruction of the family, the annihilation of traditional values. America's youth have cleaned up and are seeking family values. The children that struggled with divorce and divided homes and social deconstruction in general are striving to create stability and social order even as Ireland/EU is doing its best to bring in the destructive elements of America's eighties.

In the nineties and "noughties" MassMedia seems intent on eliminating community standards and attitudes. Where the nutty sixties and seventies focused on commonality and, God Help Us, *commune-ality*, media leaders of the new millennium seems intent on promoting individualism and social cruelty.

"Reality TV," took root in GB, which is no surprise. Britain, claiming democracy, still has its "ruling classes." These ruling classes are dominated by men, who, snatched from their mothers at the age of eight, were put into an all male society with stringent rules and a Darwinistic infrastructure. "Lord of the Flies" was a cri du coeur, with a deep social message that was sacrificed for sensationalism. "Equus," another exercise in sadomasochistic social bullying, yet another expose of an obsolete power structure. In fact, BBCAmerica's prime time offerings are repetitive exegesis of an infantilized society deeply invested is sadism, sexual violence, misogyny, murder and hopelessness all set in the bleak and endless arrays of Britain's hideous flatlands, Petri dishes of social disorder and despair which Ireland is determined to emulate.

The Government's solution is to build more prisons.
The *institution* replaced the family, beginning with arcane educational

---

[6] The "right to privacy" decision by the Supreme Court based on fallacious, perjured evidence.

systems relying heavily on Social Darwinism, ie, peer pressure and bullying, to maintain internal order. Aggression is valued. Reflection is suspect. The intelligent introvert is selected for "therapy," while aggressors are supported and advanced. Third level graduates assume power convinced that they can, or *must* sacrifice the individual to the collective good of the "State," that is, their community or clique. The opposing voice is suppressed at all costs. Third level places are severely limited in Ireland; University admissions are engineered to admit the children of the socio-political elite.

Powerlessness leads to suppression to depression, to a high suicide rate and social apathy.

This must affect the economy, the quality of work, motivations to create, strive, invent, market. Depressed economies usually end up at war. Ask the economists.

"Big Brother" and "Survivor" are based on ignoble strategies based on exclusion, wounding, lying, cheating and conduct considered "uncool" a blink of an eye ago.

Speaking of such, Holland, with its highly liberal drug laws, has the dishonor of legalizing the termination of elderly life.

In NYC where I lived for many years, space limitations create a climate of apartment-grabbing. Many elderly persons sign over their property to relatives to avoid death taxes, only to find themselves carted off to nursing homes before the ink is dry. There is a lot of "smoke" to the rumor that NY landlords are using the "Alzheimers"/"EDP" strategy to clear out elderly tenants, aided and abetted by dishonest medical technicians and political corruption. Landlords contribute heavily to the warchests of local politicians.

In the Bronx, where the bodies of aborted babies are incinerated, the statistics for childhood asthma are extraordinarily high - as if the survivors of Roe v Wade [7] cannot tolerate the forced inhalation of the ashes of their

[7] Roe vs Wade was a perjurious case brought before the Supreme Court which found in favor of allowing abortion. The Supreme Court later decided that little old ladies with rosary beads qualified as "racketeers," as the anti-Mafia RICO act was applied to pro-lifers outside abortuaries. This has since been overturned by the Supreme Court.

deceased "playmates."

If euthanasia were legalized, incinerators all over NYC would burn the bodies of the elderly day and night as nursing homes and rent subsidized apartments are emptied of long term residents and converted to luxury apartments.

In order to allow that, the elderly and the general population must be conditioned to believe that taking of one's life is a "good thing."

Here's an opinion: Suicide is bad for society at large. It is a sign of a defeated spirit. A defeated spirit reflects on the entire community, and indicates a failure of the community to function.

Historically, the suicide was excommunicated, his/her body set apart.

The *atavistic instinct* [8] is to reject the suicide and isolate or expel his/her families. This "exculpates" the greater community and reduces the risk of further losses through repeat or "copycat" actions.

In illness the body struggles and strives for health. Old age may bring infirmity, an uncomfortable reminder of our inevitable mortality but the instinct is to march on, to keep striving, to maintain independence and control of one's environment.

The condition of Irish labourers abandoned on England's streets is a strong indictment of the class system. While the Irish received the short end of the stick in the US, they were still able to earn enough to acquire property and eventually put their children through college and attain a better standard of living.

In the UK, the worst employers were "their own" - well to do dominant Irish, the descendants of the strong who stole charity food from the dying victims of the Famine and sold it for profit. Anecdotally, emigrant Irish always say the English treated them better. Nobody wanted to work for an Irish developer.

[8] Atavistic instinct© is dr.mc's term for humanity's inherited drive for survival.

Chapter I

The emigrant Irish, humility beaten into them in school and home, had few emotional or coping resources and were desperate for food and money. Many were mere children in their early teens, working on the roads, in factories, joining the army.

They put up with "no dogs/no Irish" attitudes, living in "count the cornflakes" boarding houses and rented rooms.

They made barely enough to live on, to have a smoke and a few drinks.

It was hardly surprising that the wife and children living in Ireland never heard from them.

The Post Offices closed at the week-ends.

Forget about saving. The wages barely covered the cost of shoes or an extra blanket.

America on the other hand, once enjoyed a strong Irish American community who reached out to the incoming emigrants, and set out to give them opportunity and dignity. NYC's five boroughs were full of mid-European immigrants, rich with talents, skills, culinary traditions. The Irish had few opportunities to develop these and were economically at the low end, but immigrants shared and helped one another. The educated element in other immigrant communities understood Ireland's political status and felt protective of the Irish but we also met with classism, snobbery and anti-Catholicism., but America owed their liberty to the Irish who fought with George Washington in the Revolution.

Sometimes this was at the price of their vote. The Irish vote Democrat, but the Democrats destroyed NY's Irish town, driving us out of the City and into Westchester and Long Island.

The original Ellis Island museum had an extensive Irish exhibit.

The 'revised' Ellis Island museum has all but expunged any record of the Irish presence and contribution to NYC.

Cardinal Egan is destroying a church built by Irish Famine emigrants.

New York City is now fairly hostile. Nouveau Irish immigrants puzzle and sometimes turnoff the indigenous Irish Americans and established emigrants. They are secular and strangely insular.

New York City has all but driven off the Irish community. Governor Herbert Lehman, encouraged by Eleanor Roosevelt, destroyed Irishtown, driving the Irish out of Manhattan. We are now 7%.

Despite our drumbeating on March 17th, we seem to have lost Manhattan.

CHAPTER TWO

SOCIAL AND POLITICAL SUICIDE

Dazzled by the prospect of billions of Euros, the Irish Government agreed to accept a quarter of a million immigrants. Little thought was given to the effect on the indigenous population, or the unresolved injustice to the emigrant Irish population, denied the right to vote and seldom welcomed home.

The majority of Irish citizens live abroad, denied the right to vote. Many would love to come home. Some do, but are made unwelcome, "blanked out," and either return to the host country or adapt to a lower standard of living with a fragile infrastructure.

The Irish Government has done very little to reach out to this community, with their talents and experience. We know the system and the corruption that has choked and crippled Ireland.

Strategically, the Party In Power (PIP) imports new voting blocs, becoming the "good parent" for immigrants who do not know the history and will keep them perpetually seated in the Dail.

The indigenous Irish become increasingly disenfranchised and disfunctional.

Something akin to the houses sold to "blow ins, returned emigrants." These are houses with fancy facades but "cut and paste" piping and wiring. The "blow in" spends his/her savings paying greedy incompetents to bring it up to scratch while the seller constructs a shiny new purpose-built house in the field across the road. With your money.

The smart ones leave while they still have a few pennies to their name.

Immigrants and asylum seekers are housed in specialized housing, or hotels.

Homeless Irish males are housed in hostels.

I have seen single mothers, their child, and drug addicts housed in upscale B and Bs by council agencies.

A B and B is no place to raise a child.

Tourists and visitors are encountering Ireland's social problems up close and personal and commenting to the emigrant Irish on their return. Economic self harming.

Short term solutions; long term consequences.
B and Bs were small businesses operated by women from their homes, *within their homes*. They provided incomes during dark economic times and gave women some independence and freedom. The downside was a loss of privacy. Homes were sacrificed to strangers, children were removed from their beds at night in order to accommodate unexpected visitors. B and Bs put food on the table, but what did it convey to the children about their own values and self-worth?

The Archbishop of Dublin, John Charles McQuaid had an astonishing hold over the Irish Government and was able to prevail in all sorts of areas. One was in forbidding the employment of married women.

Which left young single women alone to deal with workplace predators. In Ireland's Taliban society the woman is always wrong, so if the boss or an older male associates made overtures to the woman, or sexually harassed her, she had to keep it to herself, or be accused of "leading the predator on."

The response of Irish women to the Clinton-Lewinsky travesty was that a young twenty year old airhead could "lead on" the guy with the red button [9] briefcase.

The Irish Government does not get this feedback directly. After all, American politicians court photo ops for their Irish American constituency. It is, however, "in the face" of the Irish émigré at every social function from April to February.

[9] Redbutton authorizes deployment of heavy nuclear weaponry

Some of the comments are authentic reactions; others, disguised as questions are often subtle passive aggressive put downs, on the order of "You're from Ire- eh- land. Our maid is from Ire-eh - land. Her name is Bridget why don't you come into the kitchen and meet her."

The Irish belong in the kitchen. All the Irish maids in the US are named Bridget.

Not good for the mental health of the Irish abroad. Academics have yet to write the recent (late twentieth century) history of Irish women emigrants driven to nervous breakdowns and suicide by racist bullying in the workplace and the indifference of Irish authorities and Irish men to their suffering.

Human rights?

The immigrants that I have met in Ireland have been delightful. My problem is not with immigrants per se, but with the impact of colonies super imposed on under-populated Irish rural communities still experiencing significant emigration of its indigenous population. The numbers and rural dispersals are disturbing. Despite decades of exposes of Magdalene Laundries, pedo rings in Irish orphanages, abuses in Irish Institutions, the willingness of Irish authorities to sacrifice their own is astounding.

One small example. In rural libraries, one Eastern European will block out the days internet schedule, signing up all her friends at once. In another, it's the Mid Easterners.

When the Irish kids show up, public internet space is completely consumed by immigrants.

Returned emigrants with significant skills and experience are expected to start at entry level positions, and are frustrated by marked social exclusion. We buy new appliances only to realize they are obsolete models with covert problems. Local tradesmen blatantly overcharge for shoddy work, and *show up ad liberatum*. Women, in particular, experience marked social exclusion. Unlike the UK, where a single woman can drop into a pub for lunch, a single woman in an Irish pub is lucky to order a coffee without being hit on.

I have more often heard "I wish I never returned" than "it's great here."
And there are many great aspects to life in Ireland; the people, breathtaking countryside, beautiful air, etc., but there's little chance for enjoying it.

Returning émigrés usually bring families, leaving relatively lucrative employment for the lure of green grass and clear water.

Returning émigrés bring a treasury of education, experience, skills and outstanding accomplishments.

Ignoring and abusing that treasury is a form of social suicide.

An administration invested in ignorance will never understand its loss, but a long hard look at the social shipwreck of contemporary Ireland shows a nation in desperate need of unselfish, cogent direction.

After a few years of slurry, polluted water and land, substandard incomes, high cost of living, re-migration becomes desirable, but far more difficult and costly, especially if the émigré has returned with a family.

Foreign born immigrants receive allowances, housing assistance, etc. They also have the option of sending their money home where its buying power is five to ten times that of Ireland.

They may be able to afford designer clothing and buy cars that would not be available with the Irish Euro.

Driving through Europe in 2002, I was struck at the different purchasing powers of the Euro. In Holland, items costing E20 in Ireland were sold for E5. Identical items, not brand name vs generics.

Irish Government Ministers have a place and identity in Brussels, shared by all representatives of the multicultural EU, but they have a special welcome in the USA from the traditional Irish groups with historical links to Ireland.

Some of these groups diverted funds normally shared with cultural organizations to new political parties emerging from the violent trans-border conflict.

They may have inadvertently funded paramilitary gangsters dealing in drugs and arms. These are now an intrinsic and frightening component of Irish life. They seem to thrive in the faceless swathes of identi-kit housing estates built in a desperate attempt to turn Ireland into working class England Lite as quickly as possible.

The immigrant population never complains openly about Irish society. They accept the limitations or assistance offered by the Irish Government and get on with creating mini economic communities.

On the other hand, Nouveau Ireland is a bitter experience for many Irish émigrés trying to return.

If we, who have options, feel frustrated and helpless, how must local populations feel?

Can EU hand-outs compensate for disenfranchisement? For toxic soil? For livestock so heavily dosed with antibiotics and growth hormones that pollute even the taste of once delicious steaks and meats.

The multi level nepotism that forced many fine minds and accomplished citizens to emigrate is still in operation, doubly reinforced by EU privilege.

The high incidence of cocaine abuse, prescription psychotropes and PAS, contributes to dissociative, "out to lunch" communications, where the other party seems absent in their presence.

Another expression of the deep, unhealed wounds of the Irish Diaspora.

Comparing suicide in Traditional Ireland with Nouveau Ireland would be difficult. Trad Ireland buried its problems and internalized the guilt and shame and blame. It colored every aspect of family and social life. Communications were whispered. Nouveau Ireland treats it as someone else's problem, adopting an attitude of denial based on the omnipotence of the new economy. In neither case is there a real effort for open dialogue and ad hoc solutions.

The unquestioning introduction of Biotech industries to Ireland's virgin agrarian territories is another form of social suicide. The Farmer's Journal is choked with ads for chemicals, antibiotics, growth hormones, confirming my reactions to Irish beef. A few years ago, it was fresh and delicious; now the taste is compromised. In the West, the food supply of the poor and middle classes is heavily compromised with concentrated fructose from genetically modified corn. The lack of flavor is disguised with chili oils, at least one of which (Sudan Red) has been banned from Europe. Consequently the poor and middle classes are subjected to increased asthma, anaphylaxis (allergic responses), obesity, diabetes, *intelligence*, etc. Monsanto has compromised the corn stocks of farmers all over the US, suing them when their natural corns become compromised. I don't understand why farmers don't collectively sue them. Distance and lack of financial resources, perhaps, but the operation should be shut down: the US now has 20 varieties of corn; Mexico has over 400! The meek shall indeed inherit the earth!

I predicted the move to fuel cars with ethanol would push food prices upward. The recent agreement between the USA and Brazil further risks the compromised rain forests. We are committing global suicide, poisoning the earth at an unprecedented rate. *This must affect the collective unconsciousness.*

Driving through Ireland ten years ago, I was shocked at the number of B and B owners "flying" over the breakfast table. Seroxat (Paxil) seemed to be the drug of choice. Now cocaine has taken hold of a younger generation.

Perhaps Ireland has not changed so much, after all.

Ireland is out of control where spending is concerned; there seems to be little regulation or interest in capping inflation. Elected officials feel more at home abroad attending soirees, luncheons and photo-ops than looking up close and correcting the dire social and medical conditions affecting the quality of life of rural and inner city communities.

A woman was dead for five years. Her sister slept in bed with the decomposing corpse. She was probably under orders from her brother. Someone was benefiting from the deceased's pension. This is not far from the Knock Shrine area.
It was a tragic case. No one knew, no one cared.

Chapter II

With a significant percentage of the population "out to lunch," a system of subtle population "controls," gangsterism on the rise, rampant pedophobia, daily unaddressed sexual assaults on women, hideous, anti-social housing developments, choked access to towns and cities, an arrogant, feudal - often fatal medical system, limited social resources, rampant nepotism, and a fallacious acceptance of the "Celtic Tiger" PR campaign, Ireland has passed crisis point and is rapidly approaching meltdown. At Cannes two years ago, the word on Ireland was dire.

It's in my personal interest to smile politely and say "it's great to be back," There is a greatness about the people, rural and urban, and it's hard to remain silent when solutions are as close as the will to change, *and the will to change is absent.*

The will to change is rooted in the intent to care.

Ireland has always sent its love abroad, to Africa, the Third World. In the US the word is that "the Irish care for everyone but their own…" Schools collected money for "black babies" when the children in the West of Ireland walked for miles in freezing weather to get to school, barefoot and shoeless and dressed in the cast off clothes of their American cousins.

Collective low self esteem? National self hatred? "Us" vs "them" attitude of a grasping, privileged few? Rampant Paraholism?

These questions are beyond the scope of this book, but they must be posited and answered. If the Republic's suicide epidemic is to cease.

Suicides' greatest 'asset' is silence. Silence followed by loneliness, the loneliness of social and emotional isolation.

This will increase as the 'millenials,' raised on electronic interaction, grow and age unless they start working on social skills.

POST TRAUMATIC STRESS DISORDER IN VETERANS

The US Military's assignment of islamic psychiatrists to treat PTSD in traumatised veterans defies logic.

Given islam's established contempt for the values and traditions of the Judeo-Christian West, tand the horrendous inflicted by islamics against NATO troops, this would be analogous to assigning a sex offender to treat abused children or rape victims.

One can argue with my thesis, but not with the horrific suicide statistics coming out of the US Department of Defense.

CHAPTER THREE

SOCIAL FACTORS IN IRELAND'S HIGH SUICIDE RATE

When Ireland became a Free State , Ireland's leaders immediately signed all the oppressive and feudal English laws back into practice. English landlords were largely displaced, their homes taken over by the new Squires, the priests. The creation of a protestant style Seminary at Maynooth broke ties with European Catholicism, where the seminaries emphasized service and personal attention to the congregation. Irish Catholicism became Jansenistic, politically savvy and invested in the preservation of a social and political *status quo*, or support of the power elite.

The signing of the Maastricht treaty put huge sums of money into a corrupt system with few checks and balances. The money helped to drive the economy forward, but the Irish today are as polarized as in the sixties and seventies with a handful of mega millionaires hogging all the wealth leaving the majority struggling to get by. These boys have a huge sense of entitlement, little sense of philanthropy and no social conscience.

Immigrant earnings are not turned back to the Irish economy; the cost of living in Ireland is too darned high. Immigrant earnings are returned to the home country where the purchasing power is five to ten times that of Ireland. The indigenous Irish, working in entry level or blue collar positions cannot compete economically in their own nation.

Immigrant populations, though routinely assigned to low, entry-level positions, are arriving en masse with third level degrees and skills previously unknown in Ireland - eg, a Polish barkeep has a degree in marine archaeology. A hotel receptionist has a degree in psychology. They retain a sense of family and community, rapidly eroding in novo Ireland, where the family has always been divided and under threat. From the strong family ethos they learn to build community, to negotiate and share.

Some are fitter and more sophisticated than the host population due to gymnastic and athletic programs in East European High schools and are rapidly building strong communities despite social exclusion. They are usually well groomed and, thanks to the high exchange rate of the Euro, well dressed. Irish boutiques seem to have the same displays as the seventies. With Millennium prices. Same with furniture, bedding, etc.

The dissociation of rural communities in the face of these benign "invasions" might be comical. It would be a cheap and easy farce to ridicule the "head in the sand" attitudes of rural Ireland, but it's tragic to watch the impending extinction of Irish rural culture, and the potential extinction of the Irish people. Before condemning the self-protective dissociation observed in small country towns forced to contend with large immigrant populations suddenly dumped in their neighbourhood by a callous and indifferent NIMBY Dublin based Government, sociologists should start doing the math, as in population mapping and projections.

This is not a critique on immigrants, *per se*. They bring gifts, traditions, culture, diversity, but the rural Irish, especially in the Northwest, have been seriously neglected. The water is still Third World - requiring five minutes "boiling" to kill the E coli and other unmentionables. There are no social programs for the elderly, and a considerable percentage of the young farmers are under-socialized. Women are treated with contempt and seen as easy targets for exploitation. Local shops have been replaced by large supermarkets. These have brought in cut rates, etc., but no leniency, no "book" for those who run short before pension day. They are easily accessible by car, but the elderly have to schlep longer distances on foot in the rain, carrying heavy shopping bags. Unlike Northern Ireland, there is no mini bus service for the elderly.

Social programs are directed to the immigrant population, now displacing an indigenous population (IP) that now feels "more at home in America."

The IP has not been given supports and skills necessary to develop his/her community and integrate on an equal social level to the incoming Eastern European and Chinese colonies.

It was cruel and inhuman for the EU to expect ROI to absorb large foreign colonies in underpopulated rural areas devoid of amenities and viable infrastructures. This also applies to inner city Dublin, where the indigenous population looks sad, worn, damp-housed, fragile, dying, and the transplants sturdy and well- housed.

It was also harsh on the immigrant population.
Recently a non-citizen from a rural asylum center threw a rock through the window of a bank in a small farming town, called the Gardai and waited calmly for the police to arrive.

African prostitutes are serving the locals, drug dealing is rampant and the potential for drug, prostitution rings headed by Eurogangsters is frightening.

Instead of examining and reinforcing the elements of Irish culture of enduring value, the Irish Government contemptuously sacrificed the rural NorthWest, and inner city Dublin.

Their solution is to build more prisons to warehouse the people damaged and destroyed by their social policies.

Visiting a friend in Dublin 8, I've had my share of car thefts, break-ins, pickpockets,

The Kevin St. Gardai showed me a panel of photos of young recidivists for ID purposes.

"Did I see (recognize) anything?" they said.

"Yes," I said, flipping the pages. I see malnutrition, probably low birth weight, probable abuse, head injury, fetal alcohol syndrome." If they served time as young offenders, they were probably survivors of sexual assault or trauma.

Historical challenges to the development of family life
- Occupation by British
- Unemployment
- Emigration
- Deep rooted tradition of giving child for fostering
- Institutionalised, State sanctioned slavery [10]

- Talibanesque attitudes to women
- Church-State denial of woman's right to work, to support family
- No right to legal sanctions for abandoned wives with families
- No right to economic redress for abandoned mothers, married and single

Intrinsic threats
- Forced emigration of children to support the homestead.
- Open favoritism. Sacrifice of unfavored children to the service of the favorite.
- Children substituting for absent parents.
- Elder children raising younger siblings
- Overcrowding leading to fraternal incest
- Alcoholism and bullying
- "People pleasing approval seeking" culture leading to a climate of annihilation for girls or women conceiving out of wedlock.

Reaction to the "Unmarried mother" demonstrates the quicksand of Irish family culture.

Functional families hummed along smoothly but where a girl fell prey to sexual predators, she was doomed to a life of prisoner and became a slave to the corrupted alliance of Church and State.

Those women are still in the institutions that abused and exploited them, under the care of the same nuns, the excuse being they're "unable to live in the world now."

Those women should be immediately released and rehabilitated in unrelated institutions.

Their continued incarceration is unacceptable.

[10] *The Irish Government colluded with religious orders to prevent pregnant Irish girls from escaping their religious captors who stole and sold their babies and forced these women into slavery. They had no advocate and most are too damaged to fight for rights or compensation. Many are afraid to leave the convents and live in the world. That's the official line. Their captors are still "speaking on their behalf."*
In not removing and providing therapy for Magdalene Laundry survivors still under religious care, the Irish Government is tacitly endorsing the complete violation of civil and human rights that continued through the eighties.

CHAPTER FOUR

SENIORS AND SUICIDE

An ominous announcement appeared on the internet on March 19th to the effect that Alzheimers was on the increase. This is ominous. It's a "kite" - throw it out and see if it flies.

Alzheimers is a legitimate illness once understood as age related senility. That became non-pc so the term "Alzheimers" was switched in with attendant medications, etc. Loving family members suffer immensely when a beloved relative loses recognition, or changes personality and do everything possible to keep their loved ones at home instead of putting them in the human warehouses known as nursing homes. Sometimes that does become necessary. Given that the Medicaid pays an average of $30,000 per month per patient, in house patient care makes far more sense. The requirement that patients live alone is unfeasible. Families keeping Alzheimers patients at home should receive maximum support: they are saving the taxpayer a crippling expense and improving patient care for their loved ones.

"Dementia" is an easy excuse for apartment grabbing landlords, for greedy, property grabbing relatives, etc.

Inventors and technocrats can create comforts and solutions for infirmities. They cannot create a human person, who comes with his/her own unique history, life experience and DNA package.

It does not speak well for Western Christianity that accommodations for the elderly are not integrated into contemporary house design, maximising independence and integration. The elderly are segregated as menstruating girls once were in primitive communities. That the vast majority of nursing home residents are female exemplifies intense social prejudice against the "fourth world." [11] The EU does require modifications for persons with disabilities in new buildings. It's ironic, as the EU's Netherlands is notorious for its euthanasia program, killing elderly women off as they serve no purpose.

[11] ©drmcnamara's term for the global status of women.

Elderly women pray a lot. The Netherlands is under water. Global warming could wipe them off the map in a number of years. They need those ladies. Hurricane Katrina hit the three most corrupt states in the USA. The beautiful City of New Orleans was becoming synonymous with corruption, sensuality and voodoo. Mardi Gras will never be the same again.

I strongly advise the Netherlands to stop killing their prayer supporters.

The term Alzheimers is often misused and symptoms of malnutrition and sleep deprivation in the elderly are easily misinterpreted. When symptoms of dementia suddenly appear in older friends, my first question is: "Are you on 'medication x'?" [12] Ninety percent of the time, the answer is yes.

Another cause of misdiagnosis is alcohol abuse, which mimics the short term memory loss and irritability of Alzheimers. Many elderly people enjoy and tolerate moderate alcohol use, which can be beneficial in a supportive environment.

However, alcoholism is a different matter. My friend Mimsy, 84, would go out partying every Wednesday, be too hungover to eat on Thursday, become irritable and forgetful by Friday, and become a "crab cake" just in time for her daughters to pick her up for the week-end. After their TLC and six square meals she was mellow as a peach until the cycle started again on Wednesday. Her daughters took her home, hid the alcohol and three months later she died of a stroke. Alcohol functions as a blood thinner; to precipitously withdraw it from a long term dependent can be risky and is best done under medical advisement.

Many Seniors enjoy alcoholic beverages; it is important to support moderate alcohol intake with increased B vitamins, protein, carbohydrates and water, and to encourage social and intellectual stimulus.

The elderly must be allowed to "go gently into the good night, [13]" without coercion and fear. They must also have the choice to "rage against the dying

---

[12] *a prescription soporific/sleep medication rapidly affecting short term memory and creating symptoms similar to age related dementia.*
[13] *paraphrase of Dylan Thomas' plea to his father. "Do not go gently into the good night..."*

of the light [14]" as in the debunking of stereotypes of infirmity and social limitations of the elderly and be encouraged and affirmed in their traditions and customs. Ireland is wretched for the elderly in rural areas. Local shops are being replaced by distant supermarkets. Local councils occasionally add mini buses to serve towns already served by buses when it is the villages and hamlets that need links. Church halls are depressing and oriented to youth and sports. There must be a way of linking youth with the elderly instead of having teenage girls collecting money for corrupt regimes in Africa. Africa receives billions in aid from NGOs, etc. The Irish have always been neglected. It's that "care for everyone but their own" syndrome. It's highly paraholic and our Seniors deserve better.

Loneliness and medication are dominant factors in Senior Suicide. Some start to hoard pills over time, others just give up. Senior Suicide is probably more common than is presently realized and must be addressed.

I know two highly respectable men who admitted terminal rage toward their bedridden mothers. One said he would go into the nursing home and imagine suffocating her with a pillow. Another, a Judge, stopped short of specificity, but after declaring his hatred for his mother said how he often went into her nursing home in the wee hours and "just stared at her." His judicial status gave him access.

Seniors must be protected. They are national treasures, repositories of our history, examples of endurance. They have wisdom and experiences to share, skills to transmit to younger generations.

Agnostics may believe that suffering ends with death. Persons of Faith believe in an after-life of unity with a Divine personage. Religious servants of oppressive governments tend to reinforce the image of a stern, judgmental Deity. Labourers in the Christian vineyards preach the "gospel of peace," and invoke the compassion and mercy of Christ.

Many believe that the anguish of the soul continues into purgatory. The anguish of the survivors lasts for the rest of their lives.

[14] ibid

The devastation to those left behind is immeasurable. Bereaved family and friends struggle with undeserved guilt and bewilderment. Many erect a wall of silence to shut out society's shame and blame or ineffectuality in the face of overwhelming grief and pain at a time when they most need comfort, compassion and community support.

- Reach out.
- Be willing to listen.
- Be alert to their readiness to talk.
- Never judge, condemn or criticize.
- Do not take it personally if your kindness is not welcomed. You never know when the seed that you plant will bear fruit, or how the offer of help can touch a heart and invite a response at a later date.
- Be alert to the health of the bereaved. Many find the loss overwhelming and let their health go. Suggest a check up, and share a meal from time to time. Mourners are notorious for skipping meals. In US farming communities it is traditional to bake a pie or send cooked food around to a grieving family.
- Feel free to set limits on your support. Give what you can willingly. If you feel drained or resentful bring in a professional.

CHAPTER FIVE

Endogenous depression.

Depression is the opposite of expression. Depression is the end result of suppression of emotions. Depression is the denial of self and feeds this denial. It is different to religious self denial where individual wants and needs are sublimated and united to a greater, divine source of love, energy and inspiration and directed toward service to humanity.

The denial of depression is rooted in the fear of connecting with buried pain, loss and anger.

Untreated, unresolved issues can develop into rage, spilling over and externally manifesting - somewhat analogous to a volcano erupting. The latter response is usually accompanied by substance use or abuse; alcohol, street drugs or abreaction to prescription medicine.

Many persons suffering from depression usually live with it and bravely cope, covering up in their professional lives, and accepting social limitations.

Depression is the long term effect of anger turned inwards, of frustration, powerlessness, hopelessness.

Depression can be a normative response to long term life changing experiences; job loss with no immediate prospects; bereavement after a prolonged, exhausting illness; a sudden, inexplicable end to a committed relationship; social, civil or criminal injustice.

It can also be an indicator of hepatic or other dysfunction.

Normative depression usually responds to counseling and is an extrinsic to events and disempowering experiences, eg, job loss, schoolyard bullying, etc. Non-normative or pathological depression springs from deeper, early childhood experiences requiring curative, long term therapy.

Endogenous depression can originate during gestation. "The Secret Life of the Unborn Child" [15] is a well-researched report on the effects of gestational experience on the development, memory and mood of the developing pre-nate. The little human "lima bean" is a sponge, absorbing sounds, emotions, flavors, endocrinal changes, listening to the outside world through the muffling screen of the amniotic sac. Rejection of a child during pregnancy, malnutrition, tension and abuse can contribute to generalized endogenous depression starting in childhood and destroying the adult's chance of happiness and fulfillment.

This is not an invitation to mothers to wallow in guilt. As Third World statistics suggest, the human baby is as resilient as he/she is fragile. It is a contradiction, but not one to gamble on. Mothers need optimum support, during and after pregnancy. Love, attention and joy will counter gestational anxieties as the baby responds to an external environment of warmth, comfort and love.

Sexual "liberation" has removed such supports for gestational experience. Where Victorians were encouraged to gentle walks, embroidery, and refined foods - those who weren't pulling carts in Welsh coal mines or working 14 hour days -the modern woman is expected to maintain a career, manage a household and still take time for herself while raising a child.

Yet, "shocking" statistics emerged over Christmas of 2006, revealing high levels of suicidal ideation among new parents, the mother's being slightly higher.

Sleep deprivation is one factor. Surprise, surprise.
Hormonal fluctuations are another.
Adjusting to changing relationship dynamics while changing a diaper with one hand, warming a bottle with another, and trying to conduct an adult conversation while a tiny creature the size of a thumb squalls out-fortissimos Luciano Pavarotti and the timpani section of the NY Philharmonic takes an emotional toll.

Absent a supportive spouse, "Time for oneself" becomes less and less available and women arrive at the menopause physically and mentally exhau-

[15] *The Secret Life of the Unborn Child*

sted, socially isolated and coping with intense hormonal fluctuations.

Which is why nature provided an extended family, ie, grandparents.

Many developed nations have programs for the elderly, which are physically protective but isolating, institutional and emotionally insulting. Warehousing the elderly deprives the community at large of the gifts of experience and wisdom. Young adults are expected to "get on with it" without the support and advocacy of grandparents and great aunts and uncles. Eccentricity is no longer tolerated, but the "rights" of the elderly to a weekly bath and three meals a day has been carefully legislated.

No one has legislated their right to individualism.

On the positive side, market forces have provided "assisted living" for seniors with portfolio. (Higher incomes)

Ironically, some pagan cultures respected their elder females or matriarchs, while the Christianised West indulged in the immolation of "witches," id est, older women for many centuries, and now, sadly, indulges a culture of ignoring or suppressing the needs and opinions of the post reproductive female.

Some "witches" did indeed function as abortionists, providing abortifacient herbs to women in crisis pregnancies. A girl "was never the same" after seeing the witch: presumably "never the same" was a manifest of Post Abortion syndrome. Sterility was associated with witchcraft and demonism. It is said that Elizabeth I never married because the syphilis she allegedly inherited from her father, Henry VIII, had made her sterile, and that would have turned public suspicion of consorting with witches against her.

However, a few grey-haired witches are no excuse for suppressing and abusing an entire genderal subset.

A good word for American market forces here; for creating aids and supports for the weaknesses of old age, offering products and services that allow and enhance the lifestyle and independence of senior populations.

Despite dire physical hardship, some "Third World [16]" societies, eg.,

Malaya's Khadassans, offer superior models of inter-generational social interaction. Their suicide or "suspect" suicide statistics are consequently low, despite harsher lifestyles than that of developed societies.

In these societies life is always celebrated.

And who thought up the term "Third World," anyway.

[16] Malaya's Khadassan

CHAPTER SIX

Depression - Endogenous vs extrinsic factors

- Depression is repressed pain. *If the depression is reactive or extrinsic, as a result of bereavement or recent unemployment, for example, accept the support of friends and family. Extrinsic depression is usually short-lived.*

  Where depression is long term or generalized, i.e. of unknown or unfocused origin, work through to the source of your rage with a professional. Sometimes, a movie, TV show, even a casual remark can trigger buried emotions and bring them to the surface without conscious awareness.

- Depression is anger buried deep within a human person.

  Depression can be functional or dysfunctional depending on the extent and depth of the wounds and level of suppuration.

  The functional depressive supports his/herself, maintains reasonable family and social relations, but may find him/herself making increasingly destructive choices. Repressed anger starts spilling over, first into passive-aggressive behavior, then to overt hostility, eg., sarcasm.

  "Suppuration," ie, levels of rage and fermentation, depends largely on extrinsic factors, for example; family environment, friendships, trusted advocate, degree of choices in life, ie, education, style, occupation, etc., The support of a trusted advocate such as teacher, member of the clergy, or wise friend can make the difference between functioning depression and fomenting rage.

  Passive aggressive behavior is hostility expressed as good-will or concern; the guest who keeps spilling his drink while apologizing profusely or the ageing diva welcoming the young starlet with the words, "oh darling, what happened to you! Let me fix your make-up...oops!"

  The mother in "What about Raymond" is classical pass-agg.

Avoid toxic friends - people who make you feel worse about yourself.

If the destructive behavior is new, and your friendship has been healthy in the past, then try to speak gently with the protagonist about his/her negative behavior or hurtful remarks. He/she may open up to you. Or not. If the reaction is hostile, appreciate the fact that you tried. Don't take remarks made in pain to heart, but walk away from abuse or calmly warn your "friend" that you are about to hang up and wish him/her well.

Let go gently for both your sakes.

Depression is a biochemical vortex.

A low functioning thyroid, diseased liver, traumatic brain injury, emotional trauma release or block the release of catecholamines, mood regulators and neuron-transmitters. The mechanics are highly complex and are addressed by different classes of anti-depressants. (here describe)

- *Depression is the opposite of expression.*

    Express yourself. *Join an art class, exercise or yoga group, book or sports club. Start singing lessons, learn a musical instrument, sign up for a choir in a hospitable church… Go on a supervised wilderness expedition or survival course or horse trekking. Find the Twelve Step group that most closely meets your needs. Just sit in if you're too depressed to speak up, but keep going back. Look into your heart and connect with your longings. Fill the gaps that you find, one by one, until you can look back and wave goodbye to the pain and anger that* **holds you back from a fulfilled life. Or give it the Italian salute.**

    Develop yourself and your gifts and **keep moving forward.**

- *Depression can be the manifestation of physical disease. Consult a physician. Get a full work up before going on anti-depressives which just increase, for example, the load on a latent diseased liver or kidney.*

    It is my experience as a Homeopath that cancer is usually preceded by a period of depression, which often disappears with the manifestation of the *tumor. [17] This is consistent with the concept of genetic susceptibility combined with extrinsic triggers leading to toxic organic overload. Which of course **does not lead** to the syllogism that if most cancer patients suffer from depression, then all depressives suffer from cancer.*

- Laughter is the enemy of depression. *When confronted with cancer, the Rev. Norman Vincent Peale, bought out Hollywood's humor repertory and spent a portion of his day watching comedy takes and laughing his depression and cancer away.*

  His cancer disappeared.

WORKSHEET

- ***Expression defeats Depression.***

Q: What do I want to express?
A:

Q: How do I want to express it?
A:

Q: How may I go about this?
A:

Q: Do I have the means?
A:

Q: How may I acquire the means?
A:

Q: What are my secret dreams and ambitions?
A:

Q: If I win the lottery, I'll…
A:

Q: Can I achieve those goals/dreams/wishes without winning the lottery?
A:

Q: Do I take care of myself, my personal hygiene, my health?
A:

Q: When did I last see a dentist?
A:

Q: When do I plan on seeing one?
A:

That "gotcha" question has its place here. An infected tooth pours bacteria into the bloodstream, compromising heart and kidney function, putting the patient at risk of bacterial meningitis among other diseases. Infected, untreated dental problems can be a significant source of depression and a risk to general health, even life.

One can argue hens and eggs here; whether the depression led to personal neglect or is the result of bacteremia and incipient septicemia, but low standards of dental hygiene and personal care in rural Ireland must impact on the appalling rates of suicidal depression of young Irish males, already emasculated by the superior purchasing powers and social skills of immigrant colonies.

Something as tiny as the repair of a tooth can save a life, but dental work is treated as a luxury by successive Irish Health Ministers and dental hygiene is poorly taught or non-existence.

Mind your own business.

Care for yourself.

CHAPTER SEVEN

EARLY CHILDHOOD DYNAMICS

Children can survive poverty. They survive illness, relocation, social deprivation.

They do not thrive in the absence of love. Love requires the sacrifice of time.

They may walk, talk and sleep, but the light in their eyes goes out. Alone and "dismissed," they become watchful, fearful, withdrawn. They develop an inner world, causing a split in the personality. This split allows them to function in society while inwardly dying. They instinctively adopt a strategy of "people pleasing" enabled by the suppression of self, and often unconsciously choose to become satellites of stronger personalities, ie., bullies, wife-beaters, substance abusers, arrogant bosses, and such. Alcohol and street drugs provide instant comforts, and a false sense of empowerment as the emotionally abandoned child reaches puberty, and attains adolescent independence.

Sometimes a child functions extremely well. The "people pleasing" behavior is appealing to authority figures, eg, teachers, bosses, etc., so the initial climb up the professional ladder is relatively easy.

Until the boss wants a risk taker, and the safe world is jolted by loss of employment or replacement by the office "wild card." Or the survivor becomes aware of something missing - his soul, which he has bartered for a comfort zone, for the right not to challenge himself, to feel elation, or joy.

It is important to sensitively distinguish between an emotionally withdrawn child and a natural introvert. Highly intelligent and creative children are often natural introverts living in an enhanced personal world which she/he will express through art, music, literature, drama, or even math, science and invention.

The term "linguistic over-ride" recently became available to explain what highly intelligent children have always known, and that is, a supra level of functioning at which speech becomes extraneous and even intrusive.

It's "intuition plus." [18]

The term "linguistic over-ride" derives from California studies into higher non-verbalised functioning.

Simple example: I can find my way around new territory with little difficulty; explaining to a driver or companion how to get there ensures that we both get lost.

In my preteens I could look at a quadratic equation and give the solution on sight.. Working it out on paper was tedious and time consuming. I cannot explain the process; but in my world such gifts are more associated with threat rather than reward. I maxed a two year high school math course in a matter of weeks. A boy with such gifts would be lionized and given many opportunities and supports. My math and physics are now 90% blocked from my memory.

Contrary to the droid from Harvard, Lawrence Summers, girls do not suffer from lack of ability in science. The problem is social exclusion, schoolyard hazing, male jealousy and female intolerance. This is very painful for the adolescent who may withdraw and turn his/her anger inward. Under such conditions a male may turn to self-directed violence and become a suicide risk.

That being said, the plight of the prodigy was highlighted on Channel Four in mid-February. The focus was on the intelligence of highly gifted children and the difficulty in finding schools, but the resonance was one of profound, overwhelming loneliness.

Teachers can be rescuing angels; but they can resent the daylights out of a child who outsmarts them and takes time away from the regular classroom schedule. Parents may treat them like performing seals, or feel threatened by a challenging intelligence. There are few social peers. As soon as an eight

[18] ©dr mcnamara

Chapter VII

year old wants to discuss stylistic differences between Shakespeare and Shaw he/she becomes the playground freak. The policy of holding prodigies back for "socialization" is appalling and destructive.

Sensitive, ultra-gifted children may be labeled with the "Asperger's Syndrome" syndrome.

This creates a comfort zone in which to medically demonise a child who is wise beyond her years, or whose accomplishments exceed those of adult professionals.

"The Omen's" Damien was gifted. He was also the child of evil.

Grotesque as that movie may be to persons who love children, it made millions and played to full houses around the world.

Somewhere it touched a chord of collective superstitious fear of the prodigy.

A fear paralleled by attitudes to older women whose wisdom and knowledge bring them the opprobrium of "witchcraft" rather than respect and prosperity.

Herod destroyed all firstborn males in his territory in order to ensure that the Gifted child did not survive. He failed.

Gifted children are often emotionally neglected and treated like freakish adults, allowed to perform for the adults, but sent off to bed early. The effect is one of "always missing the party," of exclusion from peer and parent groups. In performing, he/she gives up peer socialization. On the other hand, he/she may not have the pleasure of peer support.

The performing prodigy receives applause and affection from a glamorous world - as long as he/she practices long and performs well. However, unless carefully protected, he/she will inevitably be subject to exploitation of a professional or sexual nature.

An academic prodigy creates his/her own world of reward and incentive, often in a project or creation.

To label such children or adolescents as "loners" is a grave injustice.

Most of them long for friendships and "normal" relationships, but come to realize that their worlds are different from that of their contemporaries who cannot relate to their work or mindset.

It's really cruel to hold prodigies back for "socialization." Socialization rarely occurs and they become increasingly "freaky" and frustrated. Boys may find other "geeks" and interact on projects but brilliant girls are alone, subject to social exclusion -and often jealousy - by the Math and Science boys while their female contemporaries are invested in make-up, fashion and dating and cannot or will not relate to the threatening world of Science, Tech and literature.

Females are more resilient than men and will divert/adapt in order to survive, suppressing intelligence under a ton of Mac make-up but like the fox who chews off his leg to escape from the trap, a part will always be missing.

CHAPTER EIGHT

ADDICTION/ALCOHOLISM

My work as a Homeopath has brought me in contact with many forms of addiction, a slow and painful effort by the body to destroy itself through the gradual ingestion of toxic substances.

It was interesting to confront a disease that contravened the laws of nature - the only disease that seeks to *make itself worse*.

There is a scene in an old James Bond movie where, short of a cyanide capsule, 007 tries to terminate his life by holding his breath.

He fails. The instinct to life is the human body's most powerful instinct. In its extraordinary economy it has set up powerful systems to insure our survival.

Many of those systems were misinterpreted until Dr. Samuel Hahnemann pointed out that symptoms were often *curative* expressions of disease, rather than diseases in and of themselves.

Hahnemann stopped applying ointments to skin rashes, establishing that the rash was the body's attempt to rid itself of disease entities by all means possible. He interpreted gastro intestinal responses to bad food as self-terminating systems for the elimination of toxins and understood that the body should be supported by hydration therapies, and slowly weaned back to solid foods. He and his followers did develop some of the most remarkable and fastest acting non-suppressive remedies for the relief of such sufferers.

Addiction and alcoholism however, required deeper study and treatment.

Before Freud, Breuer, Jung, Matthew Talbot (temperance candidate for canonisation) the redoubtable Bill W and Dr. Bob, the founders of AA, Dr. Samuel Hahnemann determined that *alcoholism* was a hereditary disease, and gave some suggestions to its sources.

Two hundred years later orthodoxy discovers that the allele of the alcoholic is identical to that of the cocaine addict.

In NYC in the eighties I encountered many cocaine addicts. Not having huge research grants from the NIH, my research was anecdotal and informal. However, *every single recreational cocaine dependent with whom I spoke, had an alcoholic grandparent.*

Always, there is a history of tuberculosis and diabetes in the family tree.

In fact, most experienced Homeopaths can examine a patient and make a family tree of hereditary illness for said patient.

It is difficult to find hereditary patterns of suicide, as there is a powerful embargo against the discussion of such matters within families, especially older generations. In order to avoid graveyard exclusions, suicides were often disguised as accidents.

The Irish Diaspora also challenges psychological anthropologists and archivists. Girls who found themselves pregnant took off for England before they could be abducted into the Magdalene Laundries. Again, there is every reason to suspect suicide under Ireland's legal slave trade; the damnable work conditions combined with the theft of a child would foment the desperation that might cause a woman to terminate her life.

Older Irish navvies, sleeping on the streets of London, or in hovels, after a life of labor, and exploitation "by their own," would have stories of young men who "just took off."

No one seems to be listening to those stories, and that sends a message to Irish youth, that Irish life has no value.

No one listens, because no one cares.

The Irish abroad are England's problem, America's problem, Australia's problem. They have no vote and are politically disenfranchised in Ireland. In America's cities, they are seen as vulnerable and politically unprotected (Chicago and Boston are still safe) and are subtly excluded from educatio-

nal opportunities showered on " Third World" immigrants.

Statisticians can argue as to methodology, but there is a starting point for studies into the etiology and genetic origins of the disease of alcoholism and addiction.

Psychologists and social workers may argue, with some validity, that family dysfunction generated by alcohol abuse creates the emotional matrix of the drug addict. It certainly can make a difference between endurance and recovery rates.

Conflict, anger, rage, emotional neglect, physical violence witnessed or experienced by a child on a long term basis will leave scars, often the scars of depression and powerlessness.

Alcohol collapses the small blood vessels, leading to increased flow of blood to the brain. This gives a temporary sense of power, offset, of course, by the de-oxygenating effects of alcohol.

Alcohol is, however, an established depressant, [19] often enlisted by would-be suicides, who would be alive today without it. It is a disinhibitor and aggressant. (sic)

Cocaine dessicates and destroys the mucus membranes, releasing even more blood to the brain, putting the user at the risk of stroke, cerebral haemorrhage and cardiac arrest. The sense of invincibility provided by this drug has aided despots, athletes, superstars to project an acquired charisma and to maintain aggression and high performance for extended periods.

Of course, the long term effects are lethal. It's a progressive disease.

Coaches, agents, managers, politicians, corporate heads who use or contribute to the addiction of their teams, clients or employees put lives at risk, *for very brief gain.*

[19] CDC

Earlier this year a young Irish journalist wrote casually of snorting cocaine off a toilet cistern - as if there were something chic about that.

There isn't a designer label in the world that can glamorize *that* image.

Cocaine's "downer" is allegedly even worse than heroin, known for its convulsive, emetic withdrawal symptoms. The "superpower effect wears off followed by intense depression, for which the only "cure" is more cocaine.

Anecdotally, the first hit is the best. After that, the drug is used in increasing doses in the hope of repeating the initial euphoria.

It's not going to happen. It never does. And some thug is getting very rich from the unhappiness he/she inflicts on his/her community.

Heroin, methadone, ecstasy, etc., are all toxins. The euphoria or anaesthesia which they induce are temporary, followed by withdrawal symptoms. These are alleviated only by increasing doses. The "high" soon becomes elusive and the user takes the drug just to "feel normal." All narcotics cause permanent brain damage; all have the potential to lead to early demise.

A person may initiate drug use for different reasons: curiosity, peer pressure, social conditioning, psychological escape from domestic or other pressures, impulse at a party. Whatever the inspiring cause, dependency is inevitable in the majority of users. The dependency may be short lived or may develop into the full, insidious disease of addiction.

That is, the user needs the drug *to feel normal, and derives comfort rather than pleasure from the "fix."* In other words, prolonged use destroys the brain's ability to produce or assess the need for production of catecholamines (feel good chemicals) even with the violent stimulus of say, heroin or cocaine.

Drug dependency is a slow form of suicide, destroying the will to survival in gradual or giant steps. It often leads to suicide or accidental overdose.

Chapter VIII

Sources of help are:

Twelve Step programs. While the structure is basically the same, the "flavour" is different for each group.
AA focuses on sobriety one day at a time. It has a wealth of knowledge and insight into addiction. All members struggle with the desire for alcohol and the "disease of the attitudes." There is a wealth of wisdom and courage in the AA rooms that has saved thousands of lives and families.

- *Staying off the booze is not necessarily sobriety.*
- *Alcoholism is a <u>disease of the attitudes</u>.*
- *Attitudes can change, one step at a time.*

The program offers Twelve Steps to change a dry drunk into a productive, healthy adult with a mature, responsible outlook.

Always with the caveat that the disease is omnipresent and that the desire for alcohol can overwhelm the alcoholic at any time.

That it is a sneaky disease, a snake in the pocket, ready to uncoil and strike whenever possible.

This is where the "attitudes" enter in. "Slips" are often preceded by a destructive bias, colloquially known as "stinking thinking." Negativity and pessimism are hallmarks of this. Lies and evasions are preludes to slips.

Honesty and reality are powerful aids to sobriety.

For the alcoholic, **sobriety is life**.

In NYC you can buy T shirts with all sorts of profundities - and profanities. One of my favorites is:

"The difference between an alcoholic and a drunk is, *the alcoholic is sober!*"

Alcohol abuse is associated with:

- Drunk driving

- Accidental mutilation and death of self and/or others due to drunk driving
- Spousal abuse
- Divorce
- Terrified children
- Chronic unemployment
- Chronic, terminal illness
- Irrational, violent behavior
- Public disorder
- Prison sentences for Grievious Bodily Harm
- Separation from family while serving said sentence
- Murder during a blackout
- Blackouts
- Short term memory loss
- Cirrhosis, cancer of the liver
- Suicide

I have attended open meetings of AA, and am always struck by the humor in the rooms, breaking through the clouds of pain and brightening with hope.

A recovering alcoholic makes a wonderful friend, one day at a time. The drunk is best avoided. He/she is committed to self destruction and, as a sinking ship, draws everyone under with him/her.

While the genetic aspect is well established, anger and rage are to the alcoholic as sugar is to the diabetic; toxic and addictive.

Understanding the AA program has helped me to appreciate that the sober alcoholic must always be aware that he/she is living with a ticking bomb that could take his/her life at any time. An alcoholic is twelve steps away from the dreaded slip.

AA is described as a "selfish" program. The sobering alcoholic learns to focus on sobriety and do whatever it takes to maintain it.

ALCOHOLICS ANONYMOUS - the best known and template for all Twelve Step programs.

The difference between a recovering alcoholic and a drunk is sobriety.

Chapter VIII

The drunk knows he is drunk and most drunks are haunted by the knowledge that sobriety is waiting for them in the AA Meeting Rooms.

They make a decision to continue feeding the addiction that destroys their families, careers, relationships, children, homes, and, tragically, too often ends the lives of others.

Alcoholism is a hereditary disease. It can arguably be acquired through excess social drinking, just as a high sucrose diet can trigger diabetes [20] where hereditary factors are limited.

As Homeopathy can work genetically, it could conceivably repair the flawed alleles, but the attitudinal problems and underlying depression must continue to be addressed.

AA is based on twelve steps and twelve traditions. The most powerful and important tradition is that of anonymity.

Other traditions are based on personal freedom and development. That is the freedom to choose the responsibility of sobriety. The first responsibility is the admission of powerlessness. The second is surrender to a "Higher Power," that is, "letting go and letting God." AA is not a religious program: "God" is not necessarily the Judeo Christian God; atheists and secularists may choose any "power" outside themselves. It is the surrender of the ego and control that torment the alcoholic that becomes a powerful step toward sobriety and healing.

Indirectly or directly, the meeting rooms of AA have saved hundreds of thousands of lives, not only from the slow death from self administered poison, but from the intention to do immediate and terminal violence to oneself. The process *begins* before the alcoholic steps into the rooms often as a result of a life changing event: arrest for drunk driving, domestic violence, financial

---

[20] *Monsanto has compromised Americas food chain by coercing farmers into growing their genetically modified product. Now modified corn products, including high fructose corn syrup are infecting most food sources in the USA. This is creating a subpopulation of obese, intellectually malnourished, hyperglycemic/diabetic food addicts. They are constantly hungry because they are consuming filler, not food. Depressing. Mineral rich foods are increasingly reserved for the wealthy and an intellectual elite.*

loss. Sometimes, the sight of terror in their children's eyes actually gets through to the drunk. confronted "yet again" by an out of control parent. The program recommends intensive immersion, ie, 90 meetings in 90 days in the initial withdrawal period and then regular attendance, under the guidance of a sponsor, for the rest of the alcoholic's life.

This provides a social substitute for an alcoholic who might prefer socialising in large groups to one on one intimacy and ongoing support in the face of such triggers as anniversaries, family gatherings (Thanksgiving, Christmas, non Christian celebrations, weddings, etc)

CHAPTER NINE

PRESCRIPTION ABUSE AND OTHER ADDICTIONS

In the nineties as I started to return to Ireland and drive around the exquisite countryside, staying in B and Bs for economy, I became aware of a widespread dependency on prescription medication. The proprietors were not enjoying their lives.

Some did admit their dependency on Seroxet aka Paxil, or other "little helpers," and of course couldn't "go a day without them."

The dependency of the Irish population on "tablets," is alarming. Prescriptions are readily refilled without monitoring and little attention is given to follow up care or environmental evaluation.

Seroxet (Paxil) is one of many mood enhancers routinely prescribed to the Irish public. It's manufacturer has been implicated in the cover up of its suicidal side effects. Other "mood enhancers" inflicted on an unsuspecting public include Prozac, Halcyon, Thorazine.

Other prescription addicts simply want to avoid the dangers of obtaining street drugs and Pharmatech quickly obliges. Opiate derivatives are readily available as pain killers.

As law enforcement becomes increasingly severe on addicts, prescription drugs become more desirable. It's easy to obtain a prescription for Vicodin, Oxycontin or other opiates. Once addiction is established, the prescription becomes harder to obtain so the patient starts doctor shopping, going from one to another, even changing states, ripping off prescription pads, etc., and eventually ending up in costly rehabs, or dying in ER.

The end result is a roller coaster ride leading to arrest, death, or for the lucky ones - rehab.

The lucky ones are socially and financially well to do - rock stars for example, dressing down, pretending to be one of the proles, plain ordinary folk, detox in places inaccessible to their fans; places like Britains The Priory.

Their less privileged emulators deal with tremors, convulsions, nausea, vomiting on the street or in prison cells, loss of jobs and income, etc.

Prescription abusers are usually highly intelligent and strategic in sourcing prescriptions for such narcs as Vicodin and Oxycontin, masking their desire for the drugs "feel good" effects as the need for pain relief. This makes their disease difficult to recognize and diagnose. They are usually successful professionals, with health club or athletic memberships, giving their reports of pain and injury credibility. Eyes and attitudes are revealers here; uncharacteristic irritability and flare ups are hall marks.

However, the destructive long term effects of narcotics eventually reveal the patient's abuse, as his/her life spirals downwards and eventually stops with arrest for prescription forgery, driving under the influence, domestic violence, or suicide.

It is important to leave diagnosis to professionals; unusual irritability in a work mate, for example, could have many sources, physical or environmental, eg, sleep deprivation in new parents. If you are close to the party, be present and listen. If you cannot, accept your own limitations and gently refer to a professional. Lies, deceit, strange symptoms, missing money or objects, unreliability, undesirable friends, Heavy Metal music, secrecy, extreme mood swings, intimidation, frantic demands for money are some indicators of depression or external pressures. (If your tradesman keeps piling on the costs, he may be on cocaine. Don't confront him, lose him and find a clean one.)

If you live with or work for a substance dependent person, attending Naranon can keep the emotions on an even keel and provide the insight and confirmation you need to get on with your own life. "Letting go and Letting God" may help the party concerned more than direct interference. You will also enjoy the insights of other "normal" people with more experience in dealing with the new criminality of their beloved teenager/spouse.

Enabling and infantilizing the abuser only delays recovery.

Chapter IX

Keep the focus on yourself. To obsess or follow the addict's every move is to join him in a downward spiral. If you are powerless to intervene, keep your head up and on concentrate on your own needs. He/she may eventually choose life and will need your support. Allowing the loved ones disfunctionality to ambush your career or lifestyle will create just another trainwreck.

Letting go can extremely difficult. Drugs bring your loved ones into extremely dangerous and criminal company. It is normal and natural to be worried sick, but that is letting the drugs win. You cannot change him/her. You can change yourself.

Let go, Let God and keep your life as normal as possible.

The drug addict knows he/she is sick. Every single addict that I have met in recovery has admitted that they **prayed** to be released from the addiction. *Which is probably why they reached recovery.*

While it is important not to give the addict money, if he/she is your *child feed and nourish him/her the best you can*. Feeding and nourishing the addict gives them a sense of well being. It strengthens and sustains the addict, increases resistance to disease and may eventually lessen the desire for the accursed poisons. **Help them in every way short of enabling them to obtain drugs. Do not give cash. It goes straight to the dealer**. Bullying and violence to get money are suggestive of debt and fear of the consequences of owing money to the dealer. They will connive, whine, lie, even threaten or intimidate. In which case, they lose the right to stay in your home. (Minors rights continue to age 18) Take counsel regarding reporting your concerns to the police: it may save your child's life.

Feeding your child will comfort you. It will also help the addict to survive the ravages of the destructive drugs poured in from the Middle East and South American drug lords. Should the worst occur, you will have the consolation of knowing you did your best.

A mother should never be obliged not to feed her own child. No matter how sick, how wasted that child is, the mother's instinct to nurture is one of the most powerful forces in the world.

The body of a young man was found in Dublin 8. Cause of death: heroin overdose. Cause of death: stupidity.

"Frank" was evicted from a community of recovering addicts and returned home for help. The nun in charge told his mother not even to provide food or a meal. Mother followed the nun instead of her God given instincts and refused her son food. That was the last time she saw him.

"Frank" went off drugs and a social worker found a place for him in college along with a nice flat, room mate etc. He was allowed to drink regularly, with no supports nor referral to a 12 Step Program. Alcohol triggered his disease - substance dependencies feed on one another - and he was quickly back on heroin. Went missing, found dead.

It is not clear whether the cause of death was an intentional overdose or the effects of heroin on an exhausted, eroded system.

OTHER ADDICTIONS:

STREET SUBSTANCE ABUSE

The sixties saw the beginning of a war against traditional western values aided and abetted by the influx of massive quantities of illegal drugs to the accompaniment of dire and depressing psychedelic music

It's easy to blame the breakdown of the social order on the parents, on the addict, but the drugs are weapons in a dangerous war on our culture. Mothers began to abandon their children for careers; the term "latchkey kids" was created to describe middle class children letting themselves in to empty homes to eat cookies, watch TV, sit in fear, get into trouble. In NYC laws were changed forbidding parents to leave a child under the age of fourteen home alone. Most parents are unaware of said laws.

Whether a child is well supervised or left to his/her own devices, predators are out there waiting to turn them into porn pictures, drug dealers, gang members To the druglords, every addict is a potential dealer, and the well bred addict with social access is particularly prized by drug lords.

Chapter IX

To sell drugs to children one has to have already sold one's own soul.

Street substances;

MARIJUANA; A so called "gateway" drug, acceptable in many cultures, cross bred to be ten times more potent in the third millennium than in the sixties. There is controversy as to its criminalization. Can be addictive. Is a milder hallucinogen than LCD, but long term use leads to symptoms resembling schizophrenia; paranoia, suspicion, even violence, particularly in the withdrawal phase. In NY the paranoia can also be a product of the Rockefeller laws where possession of one joint could lead to an automatic sentence of 15 years.

This is cruel and unusual punishment. These laws have been used by corrupt entities to immorally blackmail or incarcerate social activists. They must be overturned.

Marijuana has medical uses. Its prescription should be at the discretion of experienced physicians with respect to properties of species and subspecies. It blunts the moral sensibility, destroys the will and increases sensitivity to pain. It damages the long and short term memory and removes the desire to work or labor. Withdrawal symptoms can be difficult, but normally do not have the suicidal impact of say, cocaine or heroin. Where a suicide displays evidence of marijuana use it is usually in conjunction with other substances, eg, alcohol.

Public smoking is a health hazard and should be sanctioned. No one should be forced to inhale marijuana toxins. It's bad enough that so many fine young people choose to do so, but the exhalations cannot be allowed to affect others, particularly elderly depressives who might find the effects unbearable.

HASHISH
The term "Assassin" derives from Hashish. Creates temporary euphoria followed by aggression. Still used by terrorists and assassins.

Similar in action to Khat.

HEROIN has a high rate of suicide and overdose, accidental and otherwise. It has been pushed into the West mainly from Afghanistan, a seemingly insignificant nation between Iran and Pakistan. Often underestimated, the Afghans have managed to create a high-yield, ultra addictive, high cost product which turns its users into prostitutes and killers.

Heroin is a powerful weapon in the undeclared, silent war against the Christian world. It creates dependency, extreme passivity and mono focus on the next fix.

Addiction can be instant or insidious. Withdrawal symptoms physically painful and dangerous. These include convulsions, emesis, and declarations of intent to terminate the pain and discomfort. It is so destructive to the central nervous system that the addict eventually derives little pleasure from its use and takes it just to "feel normal."

The addict will inject directly into open wounds and sores, which can become gangrenous; he/she will share needles, contracting dangerous diseases such as Hepatitis C and HIV. To obtain money for their substance they will turn to prostitution, risking violent death or slow disfigurement through STDs. (Sexually Transmitted Disease such as Syphilis, Gonorrhea, etc)

He or she completely and utterly loses control of his/her life to the opium derivative known as heroin/smack/horse, etc. The internal organs corrode; the toxic filtration system of skin, liver, kidney, break down. "Overload" is stored in the liver from where it can leak at will into the bloodstream even when an addict is "clean."

Addicts and their physicians must be prepared for this, the drug equivalent of the "dry drunk." It's a mini high, followed by a low. This can be confusing to the addict and can stimulate the desire for a "fix." On the plus side, it's a purification process as the body gets rid of toxins a bit at a time. This can be anticipated, and prepared for. Counselling, NA, nutrition, vitamins and exercise can help addict onto the next plateau of serenity.

It is never clear whether the inevitable overdose of the active addict is intentional or accidental. The tissue of a heroin addict's internal organs is fragile and friable. While addiction is a suicidal state, all the addicts that I have worked with in recovery or in treatment of Hep C have stated that even while shooting up they were praying for release from this vicious drug.

They prayed. They are alive and in recovery.

Heroin is romanticized by the global music marketers, by the fashion industry and Hollywood , though in recent years Hollywood has cooled down its glamorisations of the sordid heroin industry. The movie industry has lost its share of talented young stars to the Afghanistan heroin traders.

Profits from the destruction of Western youth and family are directed into terrorist activities, traditions of cruelty and the oppression of women.

COCAINE
It is said that while the physical symptoms of withdrawal from heroin are intense, the psychological let down after the initial effects of cocaine have worn off are infinitely worse. Frequent users can develop "flat eye" syndrome and/or lose the nose bridge or septum to cocaine erosion. Escalating doses are required for effect and it is said that the user ultimately seeks to repeat the first experience; that it is never as good the second time around.

The user spends more and more money on ever increasing doses to get the elusive first high. This leads to fraud, theft, criminal activity, dealing, extortion, murder.

Cocaine's false assurance of invincibility has ended the career of many despots. It was used in religious ceremonies by Quechan (Incan) royalty and forbidden to the commoner. My Quechan sources said that its external use was permitted for the comfort of a new bride. Said source claimed that decadent use of Cocaine brought about the Spanish conquest and that ancient Quechan writings predicted that it would destroy the New World.

It's the drug of choice for politicians and movie stars intent on creating a buzz, or anxious about addressing large crowds. It's used on the sports field, giving extraordinary strength and power to the user. However, *there's always payback time.*
That is destruction of the will, the central nervous system, relationships,

family and financial stability.

Where cocaine devours the human brain, the development of innate talent and ability builds strength and endurance, character, will and ability.

It has destroyed too many of my generation and impacted heavily on social and professional life in the eighties. Thousands and thousands of families were broken up by the economic consequences of cocaine addiction; beautiful young professionals died in city emergency rooms from overdosing accidentally or otherwise; older users found themselves on the street instead of enjoying old age and young women from Ivy league schools signed on to "Escort" Service Agencies.

Professional life suffered as doctors, lawyers, stockbrokers, etc., lost interest in their clients and neglected patients and practice.

Well bred young women emulated Monica Lewinsky with bouncers, dealers, other users, just for a hit of the white powder. Lovely young girls turned to prostitution. Men left their families or were booted out.

As it was the "party drug" of the rich and infamous, there was little political will to suppress its production and supply.

That's social suicide.

Cocaine was costly. When enough children of the power elite died, the political will changed, and heroin took over again.

The drug lobby seems highly co-ordinated, manipulating the supply and demand of street drugs like a diabolical IMF.

Crack cocaine was created for the less advantaged. Instantly addictive, it has taken many lives, directly and indirectly. It also enlarged the network of desperate dealers.

Ireland is twenty years behind the times. Which gives it a fair chance of learning from the mistakes of other cultures, but it's wading in with boots on, calling "me too, my turn now!"

Chapter IX

I'll quote the average Irish American, Irish emigre in America.

"They've all gone mad."

In the first weeks of January 2007 national newspapers screamed that every single bank-note in Ireland tested positive for cocaine.

A few weeks prior one of those newspapers ran articles on the pleasures of snorting cocaine from the cisterns of public toilets.

These were written by attractive young women, probably wearing over priced designer clothing from Ireland's favorite over-priced store.

The Celtic Tiger has brought some affluence to Ireland, an affluence not backed by culture or tradition. Rigid pseudo Catholicism has been replaced by secularism and materialism. With the realization that materialism does not buy happiness, comes the desire to suppress the emptiness of life dependent on the bling of the cash register.

The saints used to find joy in the surrender of their souls to God; materialists in the surrender of their credit cards to store clerks.

Or the international terrorist driven drug cartel. With links to Irish paramilitaries. Backed by naïve or manipulative American politicians.

Methamphetamine. Another upper with devastating withdrawal symptoms. Cheaper than cocaine. Reinforces the addiction when economies, personal and national, cannot support cocaine.

NA will include addicts who found "cleanness" in prison as well as middle class kids fresh out of an expensive detox unit. Such units have waited until the medical insurance runs out before discharging the young addict with the words, "there's nothing more we can do for her/him."

"Outward Bound" programs are great in theory, but too many have exploited and abused minors paying huge sums of money for the chance to get clean.

Deaths have resulted.

It is fashionable in the US to blame parents for a child's addiction. While there may be patterns of behavior within a dysfunctional or functional family that reinforce the addiction, the mirror must be turned back on destructive messages from the media and the kitsch glamorization of drugs and drug users by a movie industry partly managed by cokeheads.

High level political corruption may also be a factor. In which case the vox populi must roar. The barbarians have breached the gates, bought into the most desirable communities, while profiting off the death and destruction of innocent, vulnerable children.

The sixties and seventies were not healthy, ultimately, not innocent, but very naïve by comparison with the post-cocaine era. It's really astonishing to consider the huge numbers of intelligent young people who elect to "try cocaine" at parties, clubs, etc. There is nothing cool, elegant or attractive in inhaling a brain bleeder off a toilet cistern.
Or in dying on the street with a needle in your arm.

Western Governments' failure to protect borders and communities from heavy drug traffickers has enabled terrorists to thrive and flourish within the West and destroyed communities, families and individual lives.

CHAPTER 10

PARAHOLISM

Paraholism is sometimes described as the "flip side" of alcoholism, the other side of the coin, so to speak.

Paraholism is complex: a subset of Stockholm Syndrome, a factor in many cases of spousal abuse, and the enabler in an alcoholics drinking life. The dynamics are similar to Battered Wife Syndrome and often crossover.

It's an insidious disease. The paraholic gives up his/her life for the active drinking/drugging partner.

Some say it started with the "first lie told to the spouse's boss." *"He isn't feeling well/he has the flu/he needs shots/his dog died/the car wont start/he has food poisoning/Spanish flu...*

The roots are usually deeper.

Why do beautiful young women stay with drunks, clean up their messes, protect and defend them, even at their own expense? Why do they endure verbal and emotional abuse, sexual rejection, social exclusion and a deteriorating life-style for the duration of their reproductive years? Why do some mothers "sacrifice" a child to the moods and tenses of an out of control parent?

The prevalence of this syndrome, statistically dominated by women, suggests a societal component to this disease. It's simplistic to trot out labels: "low self esteem," et al., but the reality is that there is little in the way of protective legislation; that "moderate" abuse, e.g., put-downs and negative humor may seem easier to put up with than generalized male harassment. A woman living alone is vulnerable to all sorts of manifestations of male hostility. Women living with men, likewise.

*And will continue to be until **self defense** becomes a standard part of the female curriculum.*

Alcoholism is a progressive, lethal disease. In the USA, 85% of female spouses stay with an active drunk; 85% of men ditch their alcoholic spouses.

Alanon is a sister program to AA and is based on the same Twelve Steps and Twelve Traditions.

Anonymity is a vital Tradition. **Everything said in "the rooms" stays in "the rooms."**

The difference between AA and Alanon is the laughter coming out of the AA rooms.

After all, the paraholic is still doing the dishes, keeping the accounts, maintaining an income, attending school conferences, helping with the homework while the alcoholic maintains his/her prerogative to socialize, which "in recovery" usually means the meeting rooms.

*Because Alcoholism is a **lethal, progressive disease**. Which gives it priority. Which requires considerable sacrifice on the part of the spouse, and children.*

Which can be worth it when the alcoholic commits to recovery.

Especially if he/she doesn't wait for a tragic event to call for sobriety.

Then the fun goes out of life, the light out of both eyes, and the spouse secretly wishes he would start drinking again.

The laughter emanating from the AA meetings is a function of pain. It's also a sign of recovery. In many ways the recovering alcoholic is emotionally stronger than the paraholic, in that he/she can, more openly express emotion and engages in a process of stringent honesty and self confrontation.

That is, emotion, not intimacy. Nor emotional intimacy. Rage is an emotion. Unless they're "isolators," alcoholics prefer groups to "one on ones." Emotional intimacy can induce claustrophobia in alcoholics raised with parental double binds and Parent-Child dynamics enduring into adulthood.

Chapter X

Where alcohol was used to suppress individual pain, its absence allows for the *expression* of authentic emotion, pain, rage, defeatism. Alcohol is a disinhibitor and frees the alcoholic to pour out a generalized rage at the world, while defeating any attempt to provide the alcohol with insights into his/her lethal dependency.

The paraholic uses internalized neuro-endocrinal systems to survive and endure.

These become "embedded" and require deeper deprogramming.
He/she may resort to prescription medications and become a pillhead, with its own symptoms and syndromes.

Alcoholism comes in many forms: closet drinkers, silent drinkers, periodics, binge drinkers, functionals, dysfunctionals, etc.

For the most part, alcoholics are social beings. They tend to prefer groups to one on ones unless well in their cups and at the repetitious stage where even their drinking buddies have abandoned them.

Paraholics seldom have the luxury of a social life. The pressure of maintaining the household and caring for the diseased alcoholic isolates the paraholic. He/she engages in fiercely protective behaviour, designed to protect the family from social stigma. S/he can become withdrawn, edgy, irritable, angry, unkempt, bitter.

However, the paraholic's determination to rescue the alcoholic only increases with his/her worsening behaviour and the "sensible" pillar of the household loses his/her connections with friends, family, colleagues. The alcoholic's behavior is the object of obsession.

Every city in the developed world will offer a meeting.

AlAnon has saved the sanity of many spouses, employees, parents, siblings and children of alcoholics, one day at a time.

After years of encountering emotionally or physically abuses spouses of alcoholics, I recommend the 90 meetings in 90 days immersion in al Anon, and the question:

How many more days/weeks/years do I want to put up with this?

The decision to leave a soul destroying alcoholic relationship should be made under guidance with a person experienced and knowledgeable in the dynamics of paraholism.

As with Stockholm Syndrome and Battered Spouse syndromes, the protagonist has implanted triggers and buttons that he/she may invoke at will.

This makes leaving very difficult. The paraholic can be subjected to guilt trips, mood changes, bizarre accusations, and the inevitable promises of change.
The paraholic will be concerned about the alcoholic's survival, easily roped back into the vortex of lies, good intentions, broken promises.

One of the most difficult processes is to return the focus of the paraholic back onto his/her self. Self-abandonment is destructive, a way of killing the self/soul without harming the body.

But the body can only take so much and eventually starts breaking down to protect the mind. For example, patients with Auto immune diseases frequently reveal a past history of prolonged emotional stress or trauma.

Part of the Stockholm Syndrome survival system is the shutting down of the ego self. You cannot be horrified or traumatized by abuse *if you do not exist*. *In acute trauma* this process may be instantaneous but is usually a gradual process, a suicide of mind and heart. The *traumatiser* becomes the focus of fear-based and obsessive attention.

For persons in recovery I recommend carrying a mirror. Every time the other party comes to mind, take out the mirror, look into it and ask what you want. Then try to obtain it for yourself. Comb your hair. Drink water. Go into a store and buy a treat.

Put the focus back on yourself. You're worth it.

You're unique.

The only one of you in the world.

AlAnon centres on serenity and returning the focus onto the "paraholic." Labels such as "enabler" oversimplify the complexity of survival with an out of control family member.

Alcoholics and addicts have lost control of their own bodies. They desperately fear social controls. To compensate, they find a gentle person with low self esteem to bully, abuse and exploit. The "gentle person with low self esteem" may have experienced such patterns in childhood and reflexively assume a parental role, lying and covering up for out of control parents.

He/she is already primed for the death dance of paraholism, or co-dependency with an alcoholic.

NA (Narcotics Anonymous) is initially more intense than AA - criminality superimposed on substance abuse can be as psychologically damaging as the substances themselves. Association with the criminal element dealing substances puts the addict, often a member of an insulated middle class upbringing, in direct contact with the most vile elements of humanity.

Tragically, the addict introduces that element into their communities and families who must then find or develop strategies to defend themselves from such.

In desperation, the addict turns to crime, first emptying the family home and accounts, and finally turning to theft, burglary, etc. The gentle child becomes a monster, holding his/her parents and family hostage to his need for a "fix."

It is easy to condemn the addict. I reserve my condemnation for the drug lords and corrupt politicians who enable them.

The Rockefeller drug laws, mandating 15 year automatic incarceration for possession of marijuana, are an abomination.

They have been used for blackmail, extortion, political strategies and posturing, and are useless against the drug trade.

On "Celebrity Get Me Out of Here," David Gest made a passing reference to China White, the "best" cocaine.

The media failed to pick it up. Gest is a Hollywood insider.

Crimes such as theft, burglary are a more likely component of the street addict than an alcoholic scrounging a drink. Naranon provides support and insight for persons whose worlds are upended by close family or social association with street addicts and the subsequent torment and confusion.

Very little has been written about Paraholism which is a variant of Stockholm Syndrome and a significant factor in Battered Wife Syndrome. Since men can also be victims of Domestic Violence, in the next chapter I will refer to it as Domestic Violence Syndrom, or DVS.

CHAPTER 11

DOMESTIC VIOLENCE

Women are perceived as the victim majority in "Domestic Violence Syndrome" but male victims should not be forgotten. Where women will resort to prescription medications or alcohol dependency, male victims are more likely to end their abuse through suicide. There are fewer supports and less understanding of their condition. The male's superior bone and muscle density and testosterone supported aggression make him an unlikely victim of female violence; where women are likely to receive support from other women, a man cannot expect any from his peers.

The persistence of the DVS patient in the perpetuation of his/her abuse is a source of frustration to family members, social workers, local police, neighbours and may be considered a "suicidal state." Sadly, society tends to support the abuser. The catchword is "she's crazy," a code used by abusers around the world. This is particularly dangerous for the post menopausal woman, 'discardable' in the misogynist millennium. Never before has the female of the species undergone such violent destruction and wholesale murder. *One million women are missing. Women are trafficked and sexually exploited in an unprecedented manner. Sex clubs thrive as women once again become objects for the pleasure of men. Elderly women are routinely euthanized in Holland. Murder by morphine is increasingly common in American hospitals.*

The Catholic church and other Christian communities, once defenders of women and the matriarchal family, have been bullied into near silence. The absence of dynamic young heterosexual priests and rise of misogynistic clergy bodes very ill for women. Our survival increasingly depends on unit, and creating a world where we have the freedom to sit on a park bench and enjoy the scenery without sexual harassment or importunity. Prior to the "feminist" eighties women enjoyed some police protections, ie, a stalker or harasser would be given the heave-ho in many Western nations. Women cannot now turn to cops for help; they are handcuffed to unwieldy, litigation conscious rule books. It's time to make self defense for girls a mandatory part of school sports programs.

I may appear harsh on Battered Woman Syndrome. (BWS) This term includes emotional abuse and bullying. As difficult as it may be for a woman to break away and reject the empty promises of "change" and "reform," it is much harder to stay and risk death or maiming - on any given day. My "harshness" is from concern and hope that victims of BWS will turn the focus on themselves and leave their abusers.

BWS is a **suicidal condition**; a slow, prolonged, covert co-operation in the destruction of the self.

Its greatest weapon is secrecy.

Its allies are lies and cover-ups.

The victim becomes protective of the bully.

The victim sacrifices one or more children to the bully.

The victim makes excuses for the bully.

The victim directs blame onto his/herself and justifies the abuse.

In a paraholic society where "blame and shame" are feared social weapons Domestic Violence thrives.

Women living on the same street recognize the signs and symptoms of domestic in one another but will never reach out or connect with one another.

DVS victims are ruled by fear and violence. They have been selected for their defensive traits; signs and symptoms of personal insecurity, low self esteem, poor parental relationships.

The predator observes, "takes note" and grooms his/her victim carefully, providing assurance, a "me and you against the world," alliance, and "protection" from "negative" friends. He/she meticulously separates his/her target from outside protections and friendships.
SO THAT WHEN THE FIRST BLOW COMES, THE VICTIM HAS NOWHERE TO GO, NO ONE TO TURN TO.

Chapter XI

He/she is in shock; the assault triggers Post Traumatic Stress Disorder. The victim goes into shock.

The assailant then apologises profusely, putting the victim off balance, still working through the mélange of guilt, fear, shame, blame, abandonment.... That have made his/her childhood a misery..

It is heartbreaking to work with them. Their determination to destroy their own lives is astonishing. You can work for weeks, finally achieving a breakthrough.

Mr/Ms self-sabotage will then find a toxic friend to reinforce all the negative messages of the abuser, now bound up in a sticky web of "spousal duty," religious obligations, "disrupting the family," etc., and your work is undone. The victim is ennobled, canonized by his/her acceptance of abuse.

This nourishes the omnipresent low self esteem, creating a dynamic of heroic martyrdom, nobility in suffering.

It also feeds into narcissism, the dark, neurotic side of emotional malnutrition.

It gives the abused a sense of power - over the therapist/social worker, then hostage to more weeks of rationalization, evasions, cover-ups, near misses.

It is tempting to walk away and leave them in the emotional quicksand to which they are addicted. It can also be tempting to wade in after them.

STOP!

The *abused* may try to transfer abuse to the therapist. This is a very dangerous time in the therapeutic process. The therapist must not allow this. The abused is observing the therapist's response, trying to replicate a model that may work in his/her reconstructed id.

The time may come for the therapist to close the door and walk away. The abused takes a certain satisfaction in thwarting the therapist's desire to help him/her. He/she can then displace his/her self contempt onto the therapist, providing his/her self a temporary respite from the self hatred and implanted criticism playing in his/her head.

The therapist may choose in good conscience to assist those patients who sincerely desire rescue and co-operate in their liberation. It's not an easy road, and small setbacks are inevitable, but absent the massive self-sabotage intrinsic to this Syndrome, it is wonderful to see individuals, and occasionally couples break free from the death spiral of domestic violence.

This cycle will not disappear until the term "domestic" is removed from spousal abuse and made a public disorder offense.

This takes the onus from the damaged, conflicted brain of the victim and puts it onto the criminal justice system.

Where children are factored in, this is probably the best option.

In NYC Family Court addresses these problems. They are supposed to be confidential, but are in fact packed with students and other strangers. Judges in the style of "Judge Judy" intimidate and bully frightened and vulnerable women. Men show up with lawyers, women appear with friends.

From my experience with patients who have gone through that system, it would not be the best model for Ireland.

Ireland needs to develop her own models for social disorders.

"Judge Judy" is a tragedy for America. She was once on NYC's Family Court. Her bullying, hectoring TV style leads me to wonder how many families were hurt or damaged while she sat on the bench. It would be a pity for Ireland to take her seriously. America doesn't. She's cheap, low level entertainment.

CHILDREN OF DOMESTIC VIOLENCE

Men and women in the death-dance of domestic violence have already lear-

Chapter XI

ned the steps, watching their parents destroy one another, as they watch in fear, hungry, lonely, tired and longing for silence and a warm, loving hug.

The request for which would most likely be met with a slap or scream.

Survivors of Family violence are marked by lack of self confidence. They quickly become targets of school and social bullies. Predatory men (and women) look for such traits as people pleasing, confrontation avoiding, rationalization of bad behavior in others, and an apologetic demeanour.

Given Ireland's social and religious history it is hardly surprising that the streets of Dublin resound with the word, "sorry."

Which is a little easier to take than "Get out my face," a NY favorite, but something in between is urgently needed.

Abuse in Irish institutions has been well established as report after report emerges of the sexual abuse of children in Irish orphanages and boarding schools.

The *emotional abuse* is yet to be addressed, but it follows from the tragic child in the religious institution down through his children to generations.

The *institutionalization* of abuse in Irish social systems continues.

Where else would the convents profiting from the abduction, enslavement of young women **be allowed to house them and receive Government aid for their keep in their declining years**.

Where else but Ireland would the opinion of the criminals regarding the well-being of their destroyed victims be sought and accepted?

Abduction, enslavement, sale of infants, are all crimes and violations of the UN Charter of Human Rights, to which Ireland was signatory.

Do I wish to see elderly nuns carted off to prisons? No way. On the other hand, for the mental health of the country, the severity of the crimes must be acknowledged.

Along with the complicity of the society that allowed such horrors to occur almost to the end of the Second Millennium.

It also contributed to the ability of paramilitaries to make people disappear. The network of fear and collusion was already in place.

Ireland had become a nation of secrets.

Of suspicions.

Of lies.

In which violence thrives and predators prosper.

On the other hand, *the lack of realistic, ad hoc support for women and men seeking to end the cycle of abuse is appalling.*

Most have children.

Children who witness cruelty, bullying, violence, disorder, the destruction of household objects, of precious memento.

They witness and experience spite, rage, hatred.

They are emotional sponges, absorbing evils not of their making.

They live in constant fear.

One is usually sacrificed to the abusive parent as a companion or personal pet. Sexual precocity manifests.

One becomes a domestic slave, constantly trying to please the parents and keep peace in the family.

Incest may become a factor.

While parents are indulging in a self-destructive death march, their children are also dying.

Chapter XI

If your child doesn't find the local drug dealer, youth gang, seducer, killer, in their teens, Mr/Ms predator will find him or her.

Ireland has little for men and women attempting to free themselves from domestic violence.

Some municipalities have social housing - for which there is a significant waiting list.

Weighed down by lawsuits, the Church seems reluctant to get involved in family involved in family issues. Health and care center offer a few leaflets and offer rooms to AA and AlAnon, an important service.

Given the incompetency of Social Services around the world to deal with this tragic condition, it may be better to take it out of the protected "Domestic" arena and treat it for what it is: violence, grievious bodily harm, etc. Legislators need to put their head around potential sanctions for the emotional abuse and psychological brainwashing that are essential components in the victimization of our more vulnerable citizens.

WORKSHEET

Q: Am I in a coercive relationship?
A:

Q: Do I need permission to "go to the store?"
A:

Q: Am I afraid of my spouse?
A:

Q: Of what?
A:

If the answer is violence or harm to you or your children, go immediately to a local police station. ***Do not protect a violent abuser.***

Psalm 91 -

If you make the Most High your dwelling - even the Lord, who is my refuge - then no harm will befall you, no disaster will come near your tent,
for He will command his angels concerning you,
to guard you in all your ways;
they will lift you up in their hands, so you will not strike your foot against a stone,
You will tread upon the lion and the cobra;
you will trample the great lion and the serpent....

There are many profound and beautiful expressions of Divine love and protection in Psalm 91 among others...

And they have been around a lot longer than you and I...

CHAPTER TWELVE

ADOLESCENCE

For an adolescent, the loss of a friend or schoolmate to suicide can be devastating.

It is difficult to write simply without being simplistic. The subject must never be trivialized, but little is available for the persons most directly affected by it - the survivors.

Teenagers are sensitive, and tend to believe that acting tough is a sign of maturity. They compete for worst parent victim status and thrive on dramatizing their lives.." Having achieved victim status, and convinced their friends they're living with Charles Manson, Cruella de Ville, or the current icon of darkness, they go home and hit up their unsuspecting, perfectly normal parents for fashion money or X boxes.

Yet, despite braces, spots and contentioius attitudes they are somehow extremely lovable and endearing.

Can we believe them? Whether Gothic "bad parent" stories are a cover for a break up or failing grades, or grounded in reality, *it is vitally important to listen in a non-judgmental way if a teenager admits to depression or suicidal ideation, especially when speaking to an adult, a "last resort" in a teen's life.*

Where a minor is concerned, it is important to convince that minor to confide in their parents, when said parents are known to be stable. If the minor is confiding in someone outside the home, that in itself is suggestive of a communication breakdown. This may not be the fault of the parent; it's often a manifest of the "latchkey" age, a desire to "protect" the parent.

It's important not to appear judgmental. Where parents are the problem, a troubled teenager may instinctively withdraw from a critical reaction and become defensive or protective on the parents' behalf, abandoning their own search for help and assurance. Do not over-react or allow your emotions to override those of a potential suicide. Be objective and nurturing. If you need to clarify or correct an adolescent, feed them first and give them time to digest their meal. Never argue with a hungry teenager.

Make sure the teenager receives regular meals. Adolescence is a time of immense growth and growth spurts, similar to the development of an infant. (Sorry guys and gals) It's a time of increased demands on the teenagers mental, physical and emotional resources, leading to skipped meals, and related mood changes. Regular meals provide stability and assurance to mind and body.

This is not easy nowadays. The nuclear family was all but dismantled in the eighties and older female members warehoused in nursing homes. The challenges of maintaining and supporting home and family now rest on the shoulders of a single woman.

Financial independence and professional advancement for women are given with one hand while family life and leisure time is taken with the other. Teenagers create their own subset families and support systems.

Sometimes the subset family is chosen for them; Drugs, prostitution, internet lures...

It may not be possible to eliminate the effects of thwarted romance, acne or other "tragic" skin blemishes. Ensuring adequate, regular nutrition for the stressed out adolescence eliminates one major source of discomposure while contributing to healthy development and maturity.

Validate the emotions; never dismiss them. If you know for a fact that an account is not accurate, it may be helpful to confront this and help the teenager work through his/her evaluation of a situation. ***Be very careful.***

C hallenges are best left to professionals.

If it something simple whereby you know the guy his girlfriend was hugging was actually a visiting cousin, then speak up and clarify the situation gently. *Never* accuse a depressed person of being delusional.

Chapter XII   79

Always be supportive. If these leads to emotional dependency or entrapment in a power game, direct your friend/family member to professional counseling or a Twelve Step Program appropriate to underlying issues and step back before you harm the teen or yourself.

The key is:
- Listen, don't dismiss
- Care, don't sneer
- Validate and affirm your adolescent.
- If the confider lacks credibility, gently refer to a professional
- If the confider becomes hostile, remain calm, understand he/she is dealing with displaced emotions, not personal to you.
- Try to diffuse anger/rage. If the response is escalation, quickly terminate the encounter as gently as possible.
- If you suspect substance abuse, tread very carefully. (more below)

Do not allow yourself to be abused. This is not good for you or the abuser. Issue a warning that you will leave of the other party does not calm down and follow through.

Drug induced rants are intended to wound. Do not take them personally. Do not allow them to wound. They are symptoms of deep pain, unresolved personal issues.

As they say in Naranon, it is not your dear friend/teenager talking. It is the vile expression of Mid Eastern toxins pushed into the West to destroy our culture, communities and our children.

These are distributed by gangsters, many of whom were/are linked to paramilitary organizations with alliances to terrorist organizations around the world. These depend on the sale of drugs to well-bred children, to inner city children, to communities across the board.

Governments have been too laissez faire with regard to the distribution of drugs to and by children.

Everything written here may apply to our teenagers.

With one essential difference.

The adult is free to change his/her life.

The adolescent is under parental control.

In a healthy family he/she may negotiate a change of rules.

A dysfunctional family may perceive negation as a threat to parental authority.

Many school guidance counselors advise parents to allow their teenager full control of their bedrooms.

This is absurd.

Basic standards of hygiene must be maintained - for the health of the household. Alien life forms and vermin are not acceptable.

Most teenagers are too busy socially or too fatigued from growth spurts to organize the sock drawer or iron their shirts, so a level of disarray is normal.

Filth isn't, and is a strong indicator of substance abuse.

There will be a level of *frisson*, friction, as parents try to hold onto their "baby" with their hearts while their heads tell them it's time to let go.

Gently.

Adolescents may be assertive and demanding, but they do not want to be out on the street, knocking on friend's doors for a place to crash.

In most Western countries by the way, and this includes Ireland, a parent is obliged to care for their child until the age of majority. (18)

In New York City, an adolescent may apply for "emancipation" at the age of 15, going to Family Court for the right to live outside the parental home. This is allowed conditional to visits with a Social Worker.

The scriptures admonish fathers "not to frustrate their children."
While it is difficult to let go, healthy parents will accept their child's maturity and encourage a spirit of independence and individuality. New ideas, an enlarging circle of friends, and the delightful companionship of the new young adult.

This is not a perfect world, however. The adolescent is subject to a new world of problems. He/she is not expected to dive in at the deep end, although bereavement can leave a teenager with a profound sense of abandonment.

He/she is navigating the scary and wonderful world of romance. Best friends start competing for the same girl/boy. This is betrayal. A beautiful, talented girl can't understand why a boyfriend rejects her. (See "beautiful, talented!) A boy wakes up with acne.

This is where a parent may be *present to an adolescent*. Sit at a table, share tea, a glass of milk, go for a walk. Don't blather on. Listen. Sit in silence, let your adolescent speak.

Listen, listen, listen.

Adolescence II

The greatest growth spurt since gestation, adolescence is a time of intense physical development and adjustment, drawing on deep physical resources, coincident with accelerated socialisation and increased demands on time and energies.

Academic requirements multiply; a social life emerges along with the need to sustain it; the adolescent may take on a job, increase extra curriculars to reinforce,e college applications, and leave his/her parents worried sick as to why he/she is sleeping so much, and is moody and irritable.

Sometimes the pressure is too intense. A real or imagined defect may cause a teenager to withdraw. He/she may develop conditioned defenses to bullying or abuse in the home or neighbourhood. These defenses are flags to "professional bullies" who can drive the adolescent into situations of extreme physical and emotional danger.

Good habits should be installed during childhood. The teenager may use his/her room as a sign of rebellion; however, while protesting loudly on behalf of their right to live with alien life forms, and keep the coffee cups curdling under the bed, most are secretly delighted when Mom decides to re-establish order in the Room of Gloom.

If this makes Mom very angry, time for counseling and she shouldn't do it, unless it's become a health hazard.

It's basically "Ms. Feminist" and "Mr. Macho's" way of showing that despite the acne and braces they still need Mom.

Sometimes, however, it is symptomatic of a deeper disorder and depression.

Messy Room syndrome is usually a phase usually lasting three months to a year.

If your teenager is simply running out to school and activities, there would be little cause for concern.

A teenager who spends his/her time holed up in a pigpen listening to Leonard Cohen or Heavy Metal, is at risk.

I bumped into a professional acquaintance one day who was hurrying home to a suicidally depressed adult child.

All he did was listen to recordings, said the worried father.

"Make sure you don't have Leonard Cohen or Kurt Cobain."

He looked me in astonishment:

"That's all he listens to. All day. Leonard Cohen."

It looked as if LC was pushing my friend to the abyss as well.

Chapter XII

At that time I was staying with a friend whose emotionally abusive boyfriend played Cohen tapes all day in an effort to drive me out.

I would escape to the Westbury for tea, which was comped by a sympathetic manager, a fellow Cohen-phobe.

Cohen's songs are not without merit. They do, however, seem to reinforce depression or depressive states in vulnerable listeners.

Heavy Metal Music is music inspired and driven by drugs. Since most of the "music" sounds more like the yowling of bad spirits, it could not be tolerated without mind-altering substances. One way or another, the influence will be destructive. The subculture is death oriented as expressed by the omnipresence of death and demonic images, skulls, etc. A teenager drawn to or indulging in Heavy Metal may already be at risk.

For every Ozzy Osbourne there is a kid that didn't make it, someone's child drawn into a milieu of drugs and death and violence. Osbourne didn't survive really. Some might even call him a "wet brain." Without his strong wife, Sharon , his survival would be compromised.

Stores serving lower income communities are flooded with t shirts bearing Heavy Metal images and messages designed to affect and infect the most vulnerable teenagers.

If your teenager is already into this, run, don't walk to a therapist.

If the therapist is condescending and treating you like a "controlling" parent, find another one. Some counselors and social workers in the child and young adult arenas may have their own agendas and unresolved issues with their parents, leading to over-identification with the young adult, and projection of hostility toward caring parents, particularly mothers.

Computer Games must be monitored. Some are great fun; others promote darkness, violence, occultism. A game called Dungeons and Dragons is associated with teenage suicide and heavily criticized by secular educators and religious alike.

You can't fight this. You *can* walk away, *with your child*.

Young adults should be as free as possible to make their own decisions **but**:

Where they are bound by dangerous influences, parents must step in on their behalf and help them find professional support.

Once the adolescent reaches majority (18 years,) parents have no further right to intervene and can only watch helplessly as their child is lured into drugs, depression and death sick, mercenary cartels.

NA will include addicts who found "cleanness" in prison as well as middle class kids fresh out of an expensive detox unit. Such units have waited until the medical insurance runs out before discharging the young addict with the words, "there's nothing more we can do for her/him."

"Outward Bound" programs are great in theory, but too many have exploited and abused minors, charging huge sums of money for the chance to get clean or die in the wilderness.

Many of these programs have been closed following death, injury or exposure of abuses.

It is fashionable in the US to blame parents for a child's addiction. While patterns of behavior within a dysfunctional or functional family may reinforce the addiction, the mirror must be turned back on destructive messages from the media and the kitsch glamorization of drugs and drug users by a movie industry partly managed by cokeheads.

ANOREXIA BULIMIA is a suicidal condition. It is highly self destructive will to self termination through starvation, but there is a payback in the attention and control generated by this disease. Its sufferer's are highly deceptive, manipulative and controlling.

They are also in great pain and unable to cope with adolescence, poor self image, powerlessness.

Chapter XII

It destroys the reproductive system and internal organs, dehydrates and damages the central nervous system.

Eating and vomiting give the illusion that the patient is in control.

But the disease is actually controlling the patient - and the patient's family and friends.

Anorexia Bulimia is in the same class as self harming and addiction and often crosses over.

It is not unusual to find A-Bs in dysfunctional and abusive relationships.

- Skipped meals/pushing around of food
- Avoidance of shared meals
- Unexplained weight loss
- Unusual dental decay (vomiting rots the teeth)
- Secretiveness
- Wearing of large, oversized clothing
- Inability to maintain body heat
- Social isolation
- Limited physical development (during puberty)

If the Anorectic is a minor, parents have an obligation to check their websites. Incredible as it may seem, some websites encourage Anorexia-Bulimia. These would be in the category of terrorists conditioning suicide bombers.

Nutritional deprivation and other binds may limit the anorectic's ability to make healthy decisions, and, if necessary, interventions must be made to save the anorectic's life - without feeding into the destructive aspects of their desperate need for attention.

This is seldom cured overnight.

"CUTTING" came to public attention in the nineties. It is possible that two or three generations of globalised drug use (prescription and illegal) have impacted genetically, damaging the neurological gene pool, affecting the ability of future generations to produce serotonin and other endorphins. (Analgesic hormones allowing the body to tolerate pain.)

"Cutting" allows for the release of powerful endorphins, creating a euphoric response to physical pain temporarily shutting down the emotional anguish.

It is the tool of the powerless; adolescent girls, battered women.

In the case of the latter, it feeds into increasingly misogynistic attitudes. Where the adolescent girl is usually treated with kid-glove concern and tenderness, the battered woman does not enjoy the same level of advocacy, and such conduct reinforces the general perception of the "crazy" female.

HOME ALONE

The movie, "Home Alone" showed a highly resourceful kid fending off assaults by a gang of violent felons.

The underlying message was that kids do OK on their own; that they learn coping skills and self-reliance.

Self reliance on the medicine chest and later, street drugs.

Tony Award winning actress, Anna Manahan, whose mother had a hundred kids (well, a large family) said that her mother was always home when she returned from school; that she always had a drink and food prepared for and that she, Anna, could not imagine coming home to an empty house.

That's progress.

A little girl and her mother were buying croissants in a bakery. The little girl tugged at her mother's skirt.
"I wish you didn't have to go to work today, Mommie."

"I don't," said the mother.

The little girl was elated.

"Oh good," she said, adding after a pause, "I wish you could work for me, Mommie."

If that's not a heart ripper. Mommie *thought* she was working for her daughter.

In adult years, where can the latchkey child "go" for internal support? To the television?

One such child, Karl, would let himself his front door after the school bus dropped him off. He'd lock all the doors, get a huge packet of the American equivalent of Mallomars, a gallon of milk, the family axe and turn on the TV. Eventually the Mallomars didn't do it for him. He quickly found street drugs.

He became a cop, heavily addicted to cocaine and ended up on psych retirement after risking a number of lives..

"Home Alone" showed a highly resourceful kid fending off assaults by a gang of violent felons.

The underlying message was that kids do OK on their own; that they learn coping skills and self-reliance.

The truth of the matter, is that they also learn to shut down emotionally, and to turn to outsiders for support, outsiders who are delighted to turn a middle class kid from a respectable family into a desperate junkie. They may learn a certain amount from the internet; but survival skills and know how are usually handed down, parent to parent or parent to child.

Child actor "Fred" approached me in the playground. He was "having a problem" he said. I barely knew him, but I listened to his problem.
It was a school holiday but his mother had to work so she shut him out of the house and he was hungry.

I gave him pizza money and observed as he made his way to the pizzeria.

Somehow Freddie made it through college and now runs a successful business with a lovely, smart wife.

Despite occasional errors of judgment, Freddie's mother, Judy, was present to her son and usually overprotective. She was a functional alcoholic who found AA. Karl's mother was a drunk who didn't.

Self reliance on the medicine chest and later, street drugs.

Tony Award winning actress, Anna Manahan, whose mother had a hundred kids (well, a large family) said that her mother was always home when she returned from school; that she always had a drink and food prepared for and that she, Anna, could not imagine coming home to an empty house.

That's progress.

A little girl and her mother were buying croissants in a bakery. The little girl tugged at her mother's skirt.
"I wish you didn't have to go to work today, Mommie."

"I don't," said the mother.

The little girl was elated.

"Oh good," she said, adding after a pause, "I wish you could work for me, Mommie."

If that's not a heart ripper. Mommie *thought* she was working for her daughter.

In adult years, where can the latchkey child "go" for internal support? To the television?

One such child would let himself his front door after the school bus dropped him off. He'd get a huge packet of the American equivalent of Mallomars, a gallon of milk, and turn on the TV.

Before sitting down, he'd lock all the doors, and put an axe by the TV lounger. He quickly found street drugs.

Chapter XII 89

He became a cop, heavily addicted to cocaine and on psych retirement following years of sitting on benches fighting the impulse to end his life with his service revolver. The service revolver connected him directly to his father, another cop.

'If Winter come, can Spring be far behind?' Pearce Bysse Shelley

The beauty of the flower can be enhanced by contrast with the weeds.
Even weeds have their purpose - the discarded and disparaged dandelion is a powerful healer.
We do not see the flower until the bud opens fully.
So too with our life and work.
If life is particularly tough right now, consider this: roses grow best - on a bed of manure!

CHAPTER THIRTEEN

HOMOSEXUALITY

The seventies were a time of social fomentation and change. They were also a time of communication and exchange but now "politically correct" legislation has effectively impaired open and honest human interaction. On the positive side homosexual men and women have some protections from violence, blackmail and verbal abuse, once part of their daily lives. On the negative side, the heterosexual community now has no protection from misogynist abuse and discrimination.

As a pioneer in the field of alternative medicine, I had the support of homosexual communities back then. Discussions were frank, open and mutually non-judgmental. Certain factors emerged from discussions that would not possible in the PC-PR directed noughties.

Two stood out: first that *every male homosexual had been subjected to molestation during childhood and early teens, often by a relative, eg., brother or uncle.*

Where the molestation had occurred at a later stage, heterosexual males sometimes experienced homosexual ideations. Initial denial was always followed by admission.

With regard to women, the dominant factor was male violence more often than sexual molestation.

A subdominant factor was coercion-seduction. A talented young Catholic teenager resigned from the national tennis circuit as the message was "put out or get out."

Such pressures are not unknown in other high stakes areas such as publishing and the entertainment industry and can be hetero or homosexual driven. The common factor in such areas is predation.

Sexual coercion is common in show biz, where stakes are extremely high. *It never guarantees stardom and probably contributes to depression-suicides by compromised B listers.*

Since the nineteen seventies, a massive campaign to "normalize" homosexuality has been underway. Homosexual activity was decriminalized, struck off the APA's [21] list of "disorders" and by the nineties, homosexuals were demanding, not only acceptance, but the "right" to marry and adopt children. The term "homosexual marriage" was deftly introduced via sympathetic articles carefully placed in a compliant media, but it does not and cannot exist. It's an invention of pr strategists, part of a huge media campaign ultimately serving the exploding pedophile industry. "Marriage" accommodates the adoption of young males and recruitment into homosexual subcultures. The manufactured concept of "homosexual marriage" is divisive and destroys sympathy and good will toward homosexuals, single or in partnership. Marriage is the union of man and woman. It transcends sexuality.

Homosexuality's culture of youth feeds directly into the continuum of alternative sexual lifestyles, S and M and pedophilia.

The campaign for homosexual "marriage" has been intense and heavily supported by Hollywood . Casting straight men as homosexuals, and obliging heterosexual actors to perform homosexual "romance" scenes satisfies two agendae. One is the perverse desire to "turn" heterosexual men, married with children being optimal. The other is deception. Just as no amount of bleach can turn Michael Jackson's skin permanently white, playing light and shadows with homosexual/hetero casting may serve the short term "we are just a different type of happy family" but will backfire dangerously when the wounded "children" of such relationships grow up and hire litigators.

Homosexuals have chosen a non-reproductive lifestyle. To allow a child to become an accessory or PC instrument is to condemn the child to a life of misery and put that child at risk of suicide.

"We know that obligatory homosexuals are caught up in unconscious adaptations to early childhood abuse and neglect and that, with insight into their earliest beginnings, they can change....But, when homosexuality takes on all

[21] American Psychiatric Association

Chapter XIII

the aspects of a political movement, it, too, becomes a war, the kind of war in which the first casualty is truth and the spoils turn out to be our own children... **In a Washington March for Gay Pride they chanted, "We're here. We're queer. And we're coming after your children.' What more do we need to know?**

Charles Socarides, MD , clinical professor of psychiatry, Albert Einstein College of Medicine.

This attitude is creating a backlash among people otherwise willing to tolerate the idiosyncracies of homosexual life.

Quentin Crisp , a flamboyant "Oscar Wilde "flamer" was replaced by groomed, tailored and psycho-analysed college grads climbing over the disabled on the "equal opportunity" ladder.

His poignant story "The Naked Civil Servant" was an account of a small boy, ignored by his father, who suddenly experienced attention from the glamorous actor touring his school. Said actor was consequently arrested for molesting one of the children, presumably Quentin, who proceeded to live a life of defiant flamboyance in a sad attempt to be left in peace.

Early editions of "The Naked Civil Servant" contain Quentin's comments on the difference between homosexuality and heterosexuality.

In the early editions, Quentin states that he observed homosexual and heterosexual relationships very closely and came to the conclusion that the homosexual relationship could never be the same.

This is has been expunged from later editions.

Quentin Crisp died alone, used and abandoned by his brother homosexuals. I saw him at the opening of a camp New York nightclub, sitting alone in a green velvet jacket, looking sad and dignified.

He had been used to generate sympathy for the decriminalization of homosexuality; once the agenda became "normalization" his candor was a liability.

The homosexual lifestyle is seldom faithful. Stability is more often accompanied by infidelity or perverse partnerships than otherwise.

The average homosexual allegedly has 2,000 partners in his/her lifetime.

That's at least 1,999 rejections and exposure to 1,999 immune systems.

The human body *cannot* sustain that level of assault.

The AIDS epidemic in Africa testifies to that.

AIDS in Africa is spread to women through marriage to male prostitutes.

Procreation is a vital part of African culture so men find a poor woman to marry and impregnate before returning to homosexual meat markets. These "meat markets" are driven by Western sex and pedo-tourists.

That their "wife" and child will inevitably die a horrible death seems of little consequence once they have proven their "manhood."

Women, of course, are the Fourth World and have no say in their treatment. They are just brood mares without rights, but with the responsibility of raising new life. [22]

Homosexuality is characterized by the cult of youth. This can be pedophilic, hebephrenic or just plain sad.

The attempt to "normalize" homosexuality prior to social dominance requires social acceptance and desirability so the human child has become the prop, the accessory *du jure* that brings the gay male into the school playground and environment.

"We're here. We're queer. **And we're coming after your children.***"*

[22] ©Deirdre McNamara *The Fourth World - women's willingness to shut up and put up. Social revolution and political correctness throw bones to women while indulging and enabling Third World dictators. Africa and other problem areas might start changing if women were empowered instead of vicious male dictators. "Women" does not mean Winnie Mandela.*

Chapter XIII

I have never allowed homosexuals to be abused in my presence. On more than one occasion I have provided refuge from liberal (yes!) harassment, but children function best with stable, married, heterosexual parents.
Children are at extremely high risk today *as **never*** before of sexual exploitation, enslavement, abuse, AIDS related Famine. Child pornography is rampant, and the internet has revealed that thousands of sick, perverse, (predominantly) men, enjoy seeing the cruelty of sadistic abuse of infants, children, teenagers.

Channel Four did a program on the adoption of older orphans. They were all so beautiful. Any parent receiving one of those children into their family would be extremely blessed.

One of the children was a rather sad boy of about eight years old desperately craving love and affection.

In his profile of the ideal family he wrote that he would like one with a silver car.

The social worker decided to make him the experimental candidate and assigned him to a homosexual couple - with a silver car.

In follow ups, adoptees were shown with their new families and the social workers had really made excellent matches.

Except for the "experimental" child. He was in a cold, rule-bound environment and it showed. He had everything but seemed depressed. The Social Workers didn't want their experiment to fail and overlooked his sadness. This was not his dream and he was shutting down. One "parent" refused to appear on camera.

No one asked why he was afraid of recognition. Did he have a record?

Children should not be subject to social experimentation or treated as a commodity. Wherever possible a child deserves a Mommy and a Daddy.

Human reproduction and survival are dependent on the subtle and

complex dynamics of heterosexual relationships.

We tamper with them at our peril.

It's astonishing that Michael Jackson, armed with a legal contract, was allowed to enter a delivery room and remove a newborn baby from its helpless mother.

He then put the infant at risk by dangling it over a balcony.

And the world still admires and defends this man. No police action was taken. No social workers dispatched. No arrests made.

There is no song or dance in the world that justifies such cruelty to a baby and its mother. It is tragic that authorities are hostage to accusations of racism and that that has more power than misogyny or genderism.

Michael Jackson *would never drag a child from a straight man's arms*.

Martin Luther King spoke of hoping his children would be judged by "the content of their character, not the color of their skin" but that's gone the way of Sunday dinner.

Liberals enamored of homosexual culture often deny the reality of high suicide rates, sexually transmitted diseases, depression, sado-masochism, emotional cruelty and violence that are deeply embedded in the subculture.

Gay fashionistas design for adolescent drag queens. Women introject the hatred of the woman's body into their own psyches. Hence the mass self starvation, anorexia-bulimia of women who have everything any heart might desire, but prefer to deny themselves food and insist on transform beautiful healthy bodies into stick insects.

The cult-of-youth focus is on genitalia and body-watching. This has filtered down to heterosexual culture, readily adopting the "meat-market" encounters presently replacing romance in a world gone mad.

The gay underworld practices strange and dark encounters with sometimes

Chapter XIII

dangerous strangers. The cult of youth is cruel, and life is harsh for young men who have not found wealthy patrons by their mid twenties.

The smart ones go into therapy. Those who cannot afford therapy, and who do not have family support, may spiral downward into fatal depression.

There are many programs for Gay Men's Health in NYC's gay youth but these require the embracing of Gay culture. Men considering transsexual operations are referred to transsexual therapists. They are not encouraged to seek neutral, patient directed, counselling.

A young man should be able to speak openly with a trained professional without being subject to legislated political agendas.

Conflict, internal pressure and the inability to share with strict or judgmental family members, contribute to depression to homosexual victims of rape or molestation.

There is nothing amusing in prison rape. It's appalling to see prison rape used as a joke or set-up in prime time sitcoms.

It's also disturbing to see Hollywood promoting unnatural sex in heterosexual scenes. It's demeaning and degrading to women, and the cause of rapidly spreading AIDS in Africa.

But it serves the agenda, the "equilibration" of Homosexual relations and activity with heterosexual norms.

This denies the adult the right to go back into childhood and work through his/her traumas with open-minded therapists and condemns the homosexual to a world of diminished returns; the inevitability of age, scarcity of sexual partners and high risk of terminal, sexual transmitted disease.

Advancing age brings deep losses: Homosexuals start losing friends and acquaintances and dealing with death in their youth. HIV/AIDS is an omnipresent concern. Where legislation provides a measure of protection against abuse, there are no guarantees in life of acceptance and affirmation from the general public.

BULLYING, OUTING

Children and adults will attract bullies for no other reason than their gentleness and civility. Territorialism in work, superior abilities, or personal insecurity will also bring out the demon in the bully.

A bully is a product of bullying. He/she redirects his/her internalized rage at his abuser toward a weaker victim whom *he/she* can control. But first he goes through a process of identification and ego reconstruction with his own victimizer as model. This masks the shattered foundations of his ego/id, replacing his personal integrity with a warped sense of incendiary power.

Institutions encourage bullying. Schools never question the "peer pressure" systems perfusing America's High Schools. Corporate chiefs may be too rarified to enjoy extreme competitive struggles on the lower floors, but Middle Management is heavily engaged in strategic battles for dominance, kicking best friends off the corporate ladders and ditching them into oblivion. Western prisons don't even offer the illusions of reform but rely on a Darwinistic system of internal control and domination of the gentler prisoner by the dominant bullies.

That prison terminology has become mainstreamed into the American entertainment industry and prisoner abuse a running joke is a frightening glimpse of the Third Millenium's empty, non Christian "Matrix" neo-pagan world and a warning to begin effective changes in values before the West is destroyed. The Christian World has been bullied for three decades now and the silencing of the Christian Voice will impact seriously on the world if continued unchecked.

A child abused in the playground will become reluctant to return to school, withdrawn, emotional, fearful. The fear may choose an outlet, eg., fear of the dark, etc. Bullies mark children who are naturally sensitive and who may have family problems, eg., recent marital break-ups. Preoccupied parents are not always alert to the first signs of withdrawal in their bullied child.

If a teacher cannot take appropriate action; if a child continues to suffer when Principals have been alerted to the situation, attorneys may solve the problem. If the bullying includes violence, assault or theft, the police may be informed, and if retaliation is threatened, police may be informed again.

The workplace is another matter. An adult may not wish to manifest "weakness" by admitting to bullying. Bullying may be engrained in the corporation, using Social Darwinism as a model. The bully may be perceived as a leader when in fact he/she is damaging trust and communication within his/her team, ultimately destroying the department. Social Darwinism may work for an aggressive short term sales drive or promotion, but it is ultimately costly and destructive.

OUTING is a form of bullying. A person is forced into a situation that he/she has already rejected. Only the party in question has the right to decide whether he/she wants the world to know his/her personal business.

SHAME Victims of abuse, e.g., survivors of child molestation, prison rape know they have been victimized. As survivors of predation and domination, they have no sense of safety in authority; parents have let them down; legislation proclaiming "prisoners rights/patients rights/nursing home residents rights" fails brutally when the intent is cosmetic and resources are not available for the necessary protections.

The "herd" instinct is powerful here; the instinctive response to victims' reports of abuse is denial, suspicion, contempt, "blame the victim."

Victims of abuse are not responsible for their abuse. They are victims. End of story. As victims they are entitled to respect and thoughtful consideration of their circumstances. Respect includes prosecution of parties committing criminal acts against them with additional penalties should the violator attempt to defame the character of his/her victim. Therapy and an aggressive litigator will be of certain comfort here.

GUILT
Survivors of tragedies, e.g. the overturning of a bus on a school trip often have to deal with "Survivor's Guilt," questioning why they were spared while their best friend was taken. Persons of Faith may frequently remind themselves that God has his reasons. Others may find resolution in counseling or group support.

PEDOPHOBIA

That is my term for "Pedophilia," but love has nothing to do with the sexual predation and abuse of young children by adults.

The sexualisation and seduction of little children is an act of hatred. A percentage of victims of childhood sexual predation become predators. Predictors exist within the family structure. Ongoing bullying, an inaccessible or domineering parent or family member, unusual stresses siphoning parental time and attention to the abuse victim, prevent healing break down trust in adult "omnipotence" and impede opportunities for recovery. A child who is left to struggle alone with the trauma of molestation quickly becomes the target of bullies and predators who are watching for the behavioral changes that the child's parents insist on ignoring. Lighting matches, risky behavior, social isolation, premature sexualisation, fears, nightmares, bedwetting, urinary infections. The destruction of childhood innocence is an act of virtual murder, destroying the child's delicate, developing ego/sense of self, and fracturing his endocrinal responses.

In its ultimate affect, untreated sexual predation damages the endocrinal system in a manner that is almost impossible to reverse. It is an assault on the child's brain, causing permanent change and damage that will torment the little victim until and unless he/she receives professional therapy or dies in jail for destroying other tiny lives.

CHAPTER FOURTEEN

AGE RELATED DEPRESSION
Golden years, silver tears

Alzheimers increasing in the US. (March 20th, 2007 MSN.com

Well, well, well. America aborted forty million citizens in thirty years. There are now too few young Americans to care for the Baby Boomers. The generation that voted for Roe vs Wade are now at risk of forcible euthanasia.

A diagnoses of Alzheimers is one way of doing it. These headlines are sometimes trial balloons checking public reactions. They say that in NY, EMS (Emergency Medical Service) ambulances are moonlighting for landlords grabbing apartments from long term elderly tenants. In the old days, you could slip a coat over your pajamas and slip into the newsagent and coffee shop of a snowy morning. Nowadays, you better make sure you're fully dressed, made up and that your socks match or you'd be at risk of the omnipresent "EDP" diagnosis. "EDP" - Emotionally Disturbed Person is a favorite catchword of the EMT, allowing for bullying, abuse and goading of patients.

Friends may die young from accident, disease or as crime victims. Death is always a shock and occasion of grief. However, as the fifties approach, friends, icons, role models start disappearing at an increasing and painful rate. The sense of loss, and loneliness is quite profound.

The onset of motor neuron disease or manifestation of latent genetic disorders such as Huntingdon's disease; the birth of a child with disabilities can stretch family resources to the point where an elderly relative feels he/she is a burden.

Limited funds, life on a pension constrict the world of the senior citizen. Changes in community, development, loss of friends, work, loneliness open the door to a potential well of depression. Social resources are stretched as unparented children grow into disorderly adults, and immigrant colonies take over social services. The white, euro-christian senior is increasingly marginalized. Third world communities are more likely to care for their

elderly in a respectful manner, their relatives supported in the West while the vilified white Euro-Christian senior with trad values is increasingly marginalized.
Three decades of "stupid whitey" movies and television have created a dangerous and

An elderly patient may feel that he/she does not want to be a burden on his/her family or is terrified of being warehoused in a nursing home and starts hoarding enough pills to terminate his/her life.

Seniors are often conned into giving up their homes and bank accounts by unscrupulous relatives who promise to move in and take care of them, but quickly ship them into the nearest nursing home once the deeds are signed.

Social workers, nursing staff, landlords and EMTs, etc., are astonishingly willing to hear and accept fabricated "symptoms" of dementia, especially when encouraged by landlords engaged in apartment "retrieval" from long term tenants.

A diagnosis of Alzheimers means a chemically restrained patient for whom the government will pay $30,000 dollars per month for minimal care.

The soaring cost of care for the elderly is not in "heroic" medicine, but in the mountain of tedious and redundant paperwork, created by and for institutions top heavy with

Costs can be slashed by decentralization and smaller group homes emphasizing independence to the maximum degree possible. Or by upping the dosage of "Dementia" prescriptions, changing any pain medication to morphine and upping the dosage.

I had to watch as morphine killed my mother as my brother was in control of her case. He is a professor of medicine who would rather undergo back surgery and never play soccer again rather than risk accepting Homeopathic treatment and proving Homeopathy works! Even if it were too late for Homeopathy to reverse her tumor, and that's not a given, it would certainly have improved the length and quality of her life.

Chapter XIV

Morphine, presently enriching the Taliban, dominates Western Medicine.

An elderly patient forced into a nursing home by a family which suddenly turned sour as soon as the ink was dry on "transferred" properties or a power of attorney may feel unwanted or in the way and decide to end it.

Few victims of the Netherland's euthanasia program are truly voluntary. Despite screenings, evaluations and other procedures, thousands of elderly men and women are put to death against their will.

That does not include persons who *cannot provide full consent of the will?*

Nor persons feeling useless, and abandoned or pressured by greedy or unscrupulous family members.

The vast majority of nursing home residents are female. Society places a low value on the gifts of women, status depending on attractiveness and reproductive abilities.

Education and family connections can obtain a temporary reprieve from the indignities of "fourth world" [23] for the privileged, but the "day of invisibility" eventually arrives for all women. Overnight, as the silver strands increase, strangers become quite rude, shop clerks ignore you to fawn over the beautiful young blonde behind you in the checkout line, men leave you to struggle with packages, when the "night before" they were opening doors, etc. Life becomes that much more difficult for women.

It is no surprise to see women disfiguring themselves with plastic surgery and dangerous diets - the Western burqa.

NY's "silk stocking" district is full of expensively coiffed, designer clad elderly women, resembling escapees from the embalmers table -

They tend to wear very bright colors. Soft colors are more flattering to older skin, but tend to get subsumed into the background.

---

[23] Fourth world©Deirdre McNamara

The bright colors announce a presence, are assertive - a survival tool.

Which should not be necessary in a democratic society.

The feminist revolution of the seventies and early eighties created intellectual networks while destroying the protective society which historically sustained blue collar and middle class women. It was anti family and silenced the voices and needs of mothers and children.

A stay-home mother no longer has a network of supportive friends. She has to tough it out alone.

Older women enjoyed shared voluntary activities with long-standing friends who looked out for one another. Any merchant disrespecting a neighbour would "know about it."

Collectivism provided support, maintained stimulus, etc., but it is devalued and emphasis placed on individualism and self reliance.

In the eighties, the great hymn Amazing Grace replaced the equally great "Gather Together by the River [24]" in film and television.

Today, too many older humans are expected to "live by bread alone." They are fed, washed and warehoused. Or "making do" in damp, unheated flats, or unmanageable homes without any hope of change or improvement.

It would be abnormal not to turn to drink under such circumstances, if only to create a temporary illusion of warmth.

In cities, parks and coffee shops can offer temporary respite from bad housing, aka, substandard living equipment.

Every day in New York, thousands of workers emerge from "rabbit warren" apartments dressed to the nines and bravely head out to work or to auditions, with a strong possibility of "catching a wave" onto a better situation and quality of life.

[24] *Check writer composers*

Chapter XIV

Or they can go to the local coffee shop for a good breakfast costing between $2 and $3, and spend the rest of the morning hanging with friends from the nabe. [25]

This is available to all classes and communities.

Small towns and rural areas offer no such hope and anonymity. America has many programs for Seniors on a local and national level, many organizations such as AARP, Elderhostel, et al. This is a two edged sword; some exploit the political power of this large voting bloc, e.g., to promote euthanasia.

The Republic of Ireland has minimal services for residents in rural areas. Northern Ireland lays on mini-busses and social activities.

A cult of secrecy has impacted on social interaction.

Attitudes to women in the Republic of Ireland. The Government debates whether to provide mini bus services for rural male drinkers hit by draconian drink-drive laws. Frail older women drag their groceries for miles in pelting rain or hitch hike to distant supermarkets. Misery, but mini buses are considered for the transport of drunks.

The wee farmer weaving his way home at 20 mph is more of a nuisance than a danger. His only real consolation and way of life is being targeted when it is the wild drug-driver, lousy roads and lack of leisure facilities that are turning the Irish into human road kill.

It would be nice to believe that Western Governments were truly concerned for public health, but failure to provide research funds and facilities for homeopathic medicine makes that concern highly suspect.

Smokers and drinkers are usually extroverts and communicators. They "gather together." Western Governments may be more concerned about collectivism.

[25] Neighbourhood

The supply of mini buses to rural communities can be the beginning of new life. The mini bus can be made available to elderly shoppers, or persons requiring medical visits or appointments.

It might even stimulate social activities, community, collectivism, *inclusion in the democratic process.*

In the USA, where independence is valued and "giving up control" means just that - any weakness can bring one to a "soylent green" scenario where a huge meat grinder of social workers and prescription happy "just made it thru college" interns are more than happy to make momentous, life changing decisions for complete strangers. It's no surprise to encounter increasing numbers of well educated Americans admitting to hoarding pills so that they will not fall into the hands of experimental medicine.

Here are some encounters with relative strangers;

I met "Nash" in the deli where he was buying soup for his mother who was confined to a nursing home after her husband died and " Nash" and his boyfriend took over their luxury apartment and moved her out.

I sent my best wishes to his mother, whom I had known for many years. "Nash" started to speak about "useless eaters," how he had his pills lined up for when his faculties started to fade.

"Your mother would be considered a "useless eater:" yet you visit her every day and bring nourishing foods to her."

"That's different," he said.

"Life is a gift. Each person is unique and special."

Three months later, his mother was dead.

"Lana" is in her eighties and still dancing. Supple as a willow twig and highly alert, she contacted a suicide promoting organization for information how to "stay in control" if she fell ill.

Chapter XIV

She couldn't bear to be attached to machines, she said.

Understandable; as a dancer, physical freedom is vital to her emotional health.

I asked if she had ever experienced illness. She said "no."

I asked if she were aware that sick people fought for recovery, that the body took over.

She looked at me as if I were nuts and moved further down the subway platform.

I've met her several times since. We always discuss ballet.

ECONOMIC FACTORS

The Great Depression [26] was allegedly brought about when JP Morgan looked out on the Marina where his magnificent yacht was surrounded by other magnificent yachts and decided it was too crowded. To reduce the number of millionaires in America he dumped his stock triggering a free-fall which sends shudders through stock market mavens today.

The weeks that followed were followed were marked by the "new poor" - hardworking Americans standing in breadlines. Former millionaires jumped from window ledges in the Financial District, certain they would never recoup their losses or pay off debt accumulations.

While recovery of original status was questionable, patience would have allowed them to see an improvement in the economy, the beginning of recovery.

This was a result of work programs established by Franklin Delano Roosevelt who launched a series of projects across the nation, for the beauty and betterment of America.

[26] *The period following the fall of the Stock Market in 1929.*

It worked! Employment empowered the people and the new trickle of money allowed small business to stay open, which in turn generated more money, more employment and the expansion of towns into cities.

America produced some of the finest artists, performers, engineers and architects in its history.

And the suicide rate plummeted.

There is no benign rescuer such as President Roosevelt for individuals burdened by debt. The new usurers, credit card pushers, are poorly regulated in many domains and are taking advantage of new prosperities. They offer increasing credit loads to persons with little or no experience in money management, increasing the load until the client is choked and crippled with debt.

They are strategised to pounce on every loophole and weakness in a client's paying habits, and impose cruel interest rates for lay payments.

They are absolutely merciless and treat a client dealing with recent unemployment or terminal disease just as abusively as a self-indulgent shopper or compulsive gambler.

They are set up to maximize and penalize error, disrupting family meals with hostile demands for payments.

Debt collecting has to be one of the cruelest jobs in the world, and the person who enjoys it would have a sadistic component to his/her personality.

Tactics employed by credit card companies would probably not be permitted in Abu Ghraib.

A dysfunctional family copes by not engaging.

A functional individual, new to crisis, may try to negotiate or engage, meeting with ridicule and abuse.

Eventually, the functional individual gives up and becomes dysfunctional.

An individual burdened by debt can become suicidal.

It would be very interesting if abused debtors united to withhold payments in, say, March.

They would have to be prepared to pay extra in April, but the credit industry might get the message and review its tactics.

Where self-regulation fails, legislation can step in and limit offensive and dangerous tactics by debt collectors.

Instead of being pushed to the breaking point, allow the bank to do the work and pay a reasonable amount out of direct debit. This will take pressure off, release time and energy for a personal and professional life, and allow the debtor to gain control and move forward.

Where the problem is financial; ie, loss of income, inability to pay in full, pay the interest, **plus**.

Paying interest just gets the jackals off your back. Paying interest plus whatever you can afford, will eventually pay down the debt.

It's better to pay small amounts on a regular basis than a large, incomplete sum, followed by gaps in the payment schedule. The debt and interest multiply like giant bunnies and you're worse off than if you'd spent your lump sum on a new car or fur coat.

Some cards offer insurance for sudden loss of employment, disability, etc. This does not automatically kick in and you have to apply, with paperwork in order to qualify for coverage.

While there is life, there is hope. Debts can be repaid over time. Overtime legislation can be brought in to limit abusive practices by the usury business which has developed sophisticated strategies for keeping debtors in debt. There are no allowances for catastrophic situations such as war, civil and human rights violations, terminal illness, etc.

Where Government Revenue and Taxes are concerned, hire professionals to represent you. "Free" legal clinics are often stretched to the limit, offering limited time per client, while Internal Revenue departments enjoy permanent care and representation by an army of professionals.

Money can be come by. Money can be made. Fortunes can be lost and found.

Nothing replaces the unique individual that is you.

After all, there is only one of you.

CHAPTER FIFTEEN

PHYSICAL ILLNESSES ASSOCIATED WITH DEPRESSION

Almost any infection can cause depression of one degree or another. Bacteria from an infected tooth can leach into the bloodstream, overloading organs of filtration and excretion, and circulating in the brain.

The effect of potentially lethal, antibiotic resistant infections such as AIDS and Syphilis which attack the Central Nervous System can be devastating to a patient.
Flu, auto-immune disease, viral disease, mononucleosis, ulcerative colitis, hepatitis, pneumonias all will inevitably impact on a patient's mental health.

Neurological disorders such as Parkinson, MS or brain tumors can be devastating. Depression markedly follows stroke victims, and is difficult to treat.

Hormonal disorders - PMS, Addison's, Cushings, thyroid malfunctions, all challenge the brightest of patients.

Insomnia must always be investigated, as, uncorrected, it will lead to depression. Drugs are best avoided; alternative therapies and/or psychotherapy are beneficial without leading to dependency or symptoms of Alzheimers.

Drugs, malnutrition, etc.

So, a thorough check-up, healthy diet and exercise prevent many of the above, and/or promote rapid recovery in some.

As rehabilitation therapists have proven time and time again, it's never too late to start.

A little coffee is good; the B6 in roasted coffee beans is probably beneficial to, say, a patient with Parkinsons. It may be contra-indicated so check with your physician and or a reputable nutritionist.

CHRONIC ILLNESS

Supported or unsupported, chronic illness can wear on the spirit.

It can also deepen and mature the character as the mind accepts limitations and transforms aggression to gentleness, empathy and patience.

The diagnosis of a terminal illness can send shock waves through an individual or family.

A diagnoses of terminal illness does not necessarily mean death. Miracles happen more often than we think; diagnoses "miraculously" prove inaccurate. This usually means the patient has seen a homeopath - or an angel.

Having seen a multitude of "spontaneous recoveries" in my homeopathic practice I wonder how many such recoveries are attributable to homeopathic intervention.

No other medicine works as deeply as ours in searching out and eradicating the origin or "exciting cause" of disease.

Prayer, Distance healing, Laying on of hands can also flout conventional medical wisdom.

It is better to tell your physician that you are using alternatives. They are usually well disposed to homeopathy even if few of them actually *understand it*. Enlightened physicians should be able to advise or caution with regard to some of the extremes of complementary therapies.

And weird foods. Such as massive amounts of blue algae, concentrated hydrogen peroxide injections, etc., *high fructose corn syrup*. Empty, potentially diabetes inducing food filler.

Assuming the diagnoses is correct and the prognosis negative, a person of Faith will immediately seek spiritual counsel.

An agnostic will probably seek a secular therapist.

Chapter XV

The body has betrayed you, decided to malfunction, to shut down. Sometimes we've betrayed the body; cigarettes, drugs, alcohol, sedentary habits, inadequate or inappropriate nutrition, foreign diseases, fat diets…

Amazing what the human body endures before we say
"Enough!"

Be kind to your body. It's the only one you'll ever have. It's your connection to your mother, your father, your ancestors. It's the executor of the mind.

Keep it clean.

Keep it nourished.

Keep it strong.

Eat and drink well and exercise. Build strength into it with good foods and as much fresh air as you can take.
Townies, get away from the carbon monoxide and walk by the sea.

If you are ill and confined to bed, that can be a very close and rewarding encounter with grace, an opportunity for stillness, for life review, for unity with the Lord.

Many great artists and saints suffered from prolonged ill health.

As if the mind and spirit were too strong for their physical constraints.

Which may be true in one respect; in another, malnutrition played a very strong role.

Despite intense suffering, most persevere, and ultimately, triumph.

"Comfort ye my people, thus says the Lord!" Isaiah

The Psalms are gentle, profound reminders of our relationship with God and His love for us. Comfort indeed!
King David is referred to as the Psalmist, and the Psalms are primarily attributed to him.
David knew the love of the Lord intimately because he did some pretty bad things, such as putting a general in the front line so he could have relations with his wife, but the Lord forgave him.
For those carrying a burden of guilt or shame, read the Psalms, and turn the suffering and sorrow over to God.

In no particular order, here are a few lines from the Psalms that we found and prayed aloud on 9/11 as the rescuers were risking and giving their lives to save others. The death toll was expected to be 25,000, but was ultimately just over 3,000. That means that there were **22,000 miracles** on the morning of 9/11, 2000!

Psalm 91 - He who dwells in the shelter of the Most High will rest in the shelter of the Almighty...*the shelter of the Almighty*... It sounds like a good place to be, but there's so much more in that Psalm, "I will protect him," "I will answer him," "I will be with him in trouble..." That promise is to all who call on His name...

Psalm 23 - The most famous of all, "The Lord is my Shepherd, I'll not want. It goes on to describe green pastures, cool waters, anointing with oil...lush, gentle, generous...beautiful...

Psalm 139 - Are you lonely? Because this psalm assures us that we are not alone: "Oh Lord, you have searched me and you know me. You know when I sit and when I stand..."

Treat yourself to a book of Psalms, and open it with trust and faith that you will be guided to the words most healing for you.

Be Comforted.

CHAPTER SIXTEEN

TRAUMATIC BRAIN INJURY (TBI)

The emotional impact of Traumatic Brain Injury is often underestimated. It's a complex subject, requiring its own extended treatment. It is included here for its often neglected sidebar of depression, frustration due to loss of skills, hopelessness and potential for suicide.

Obvious brain trauma, eg, fractured skull, stroke, aneurysms visible on CT scans are usually treated with aggressive therapies.

Any injury or trauma can affect mood and emotion. The loss of a limb, cognitive function or one of the five senses can disorient or depress the strongest of persons. Therapy or Counseling is always a good idea. Shock accompanies surgical injury just as it will an accident. Withdrawal from anesthesia is seldom considered a factor in post-op depressions, but it's almost inevitable considering the toxic overload on the liver and other organs of filtration and elimination.

Traumatic Brain Injury survivors and families can be surprised at the mood altering effects of some Brain Injuries; those affecting the amygdala and hypothalamus in particular. These can be extreme, ranging from suicidal depression to violent rage. These are usually self-limiting, often ceasing as abruptly as they begin.

The patient should not be judged or ridiculed. TBI is a tragedy and requires support, understanding and counseling. The patient must be reassured that the mood swings are temporary, and given soothing actions or calming triggers to get through it.

Violence, of course, should not be tolerated. A person who is so damaged that he/she cannot control violent actions needs professional intervention. Others may have some measure of control, but find that control a challenge.

Persons with visible injuries often have a struggle with public perception, but the TBI cannot offer visual cues as to his/her impediments. Slow or difficult speech can be irritating to the intolerant, difficult comprehension and retention may invoke contempt or discourtesy, leading to frustration and irritability. That is not necessarily a result of neurons misfiring, but a normal reaction to personalized cruelty.

Without support, the struggle to regain mental functions, combined with injury related depression and anxiety can lead to suicidal ideations. These must always be taken seriously.

TBI is a complex subject requiring its own book. While I cannot do it justice here, post TBI depressions can be powerful. Persons with TBI and their families require support, encouragement and rehab as *symptoms can improve dramatically with the right care.*

The emotional impact of Traumatic Brain Injury is often underestimated but it's a complex subject, requiring its own extended treatment. It is included for its often neglected sidebar of depression, frustration due to loss of skills, hopelessness and potential for suicide.

Obvious brain trauma, eg, fractured skull, stroke, aneurysms visible on CT scans are usually treated with aggressive therapies.

Physiotherapy helps to repair atrophied or paralysed muscles, and re establish neural pathways.

Psychotherapy can help the TBI patient with issues such as loss of skills, independence, etc.

Subdural bleeds may not show up on CT scans and the TBI patient discharged with an advice sheet.

Which is fine if there is an intelligent adult in the mix to observe the patient for 72 hours.

The effects of TBI can manifest for years.

Chapter XVI

These include: loss of memory
 Mood swings
 Short Term memory loss
 Amnesia
 Depression
 Sense of Loss of Control
 Loss of communication skills
 Scrambled speech
 Attention deficit disorder
 Inability to concentrate, complete tasks or, for example, do taxes.
 Loss of consciousness
 Seizures
 A profound sense of loss, of something missing.

Loss of credibility. The TBI "label" can destroy a reputation in three seconds flat.

Economic consequences can lead to malnutrition, leading to misinterpretation of symptoms.

In other words, a patient who faints from hunger or collapses after an extensive "glycogen stealing" work out is probably *not* having a seizure and just needs nutritional therapy, ie, a good meal.

TBI patients need support and encouragement, not criticism or ridicule.

They may require help re-establishing order, maintaining a check-book, etc., or confidence building reading exercises where speech has been impacted. This may require repetition. If it's painful or frustrating, or similar to teaching a relative to drive, let someone else do it and save your time together for de-stressing, uplifting experiences.

Patience and kindness are the best healers in such cases. Build happy memories.

Depending on location and severity of injury a TBI patient can manifest irritability or frustration or rage. This may be due to misfiring neurons, fear or frustration, but it is important not to reinforce abusive behavior, should it occur.

Calmly state that you're leaving and will return when the patient/loved one is calmer.

If necessary, follow through on the warning. Never criticize, ridicule or browbeat a TBI patient.

The TBI patient has a right to privacy. The unsteady gait, difficult mental focus and linguistic problems of brain lesions, tumors, cysts and traumas can manifest as inebriation or drunkenness. A diabetic can appear to be inebriated just prior to collapsing into coma. It is better not to judge until tests are completed.

Don't feel you have to make excuses or "explain" such behavior to strangers no matter how curious or critical.

It's none of their business, unless, for example, Uncle Joe has spilled coffee on someone's lap.

TBI can become a label and liability. Ill- meaning persons may use that as an excuse to provoke a confrontation or challenge the patient. A cost-cutting, ethically challenged boss may use that as an excuse to fire a good worker whose challenges make *him* uncomfortable.

There are some very sick and sadistic people in the wide world. Too many are employed in hospitals, undoing the good work of the "angels," putting patients at risk and setting up their bosses for litigation.

Best avoided.

CHAPTER SEVENTEEN

WOMENS' ISSUES - POST ABORTION SYNDROME

In the last millennium, schools graduated well mannered, well lettered teenagers, buttoned up emotionally and sartorially.

They were fastidious in appearance, and "polite to their elders." They planned a family, and saved toward a house and home prior to marriage.

The social revolution of the sixties changed all that. Drugs created a lethargy and indifference to standards of behaviour and hygiene.

Language and attitudes once extremely marginalized entered mainstream dialogue and romance flew out the window.

Girls who once insisted on being wooed and courted with flowers, formal dates, and gifts of quality or thoughtfulness would be horrified at the lubriciousness of today's world, where young women are delighted when Mr. Second time around asks them to give up their youth and beauty to live with him and wash his socks.

These are beautiful young women with graduate degrees and zero self esteem.

In Ireland I was struck by the number of attractive young women presenting as "zoners," contiguously absent and present.

47% of Irish women have had abortions.

Almost half the female population is suffering from Post Abortion Syndrome, latent or manifest.

The loss of a child through spontaneous miscarriage or stillbirth is an underestimated trauma, similar to PAS, but absent the terrible burden of guilt.

CURA or dedicated clergy can make referrals for Post Abortion Syndrome (PAS) counseling. Some retreats are dedicated to healing the wound of abortion.

Mothers are encouraged to give their baby a name; to speak about their hopes, dreams and fears; to express their sorrow and profound sense of loss.

Where the loss of a child is spontaneous abortion or stillbirth, similar healing is offered with some differences.

PAS counseling cannot bring your baby back but it can restore a woman's self esteem.

A woman may resort to abortion to protect a high-flying career.

Allowing herself to conceive suggests that the high-flying career was not enough.

There are many reasons for a woman to consider/be driven to abortion.

Everyone of them suggest something was missing from the start.

At pro life meetings, it is easy to spot fathers who wanted their babies, offered marriage and support, but were unable to save their child.

There is a bleakness, cynicism and absence of joy in their eyes.

A father's fundamental instinct to protect his child is destroyed by abortion.

On the other hand, fathering a child out of wedlock may suggest a willingness to exploit women, a lack of understanding or absence of respect for gift of fatherhood.

Science has made a mockery of the human body. It is no longer "the image and likeness of God," or the "temple of the Holy Spirit."

The human body has become a commodity to be "harvested," spliced, transplanted, transgendered, transgenomed, transgressed.

Chapter XVII

The latest body part to hit the transplant list is the uterus. Now, prisoners in China are mutilated prior to execution, their bodies butchered while they are alive and well, in order to provide organs for well to do foreigners.

In India and the Third World, poor people are persuaded to sell their kidneys, and are subjected to quickie operations in unsanitary conditions, and left to recover untreated; in pain, with infection and profound loss of quality of life.

In the US, doctors keep patients on life support and "harvest" parts from still living bodies. They will provide a lot of jargon re viability, non viability, etc., but the fundamental fact of the matter is the entire world is suffering from a collective Post Abortion Syndrome, a profound loss of respect for Human Life.

If you can destroy pre-natal life, barbarically dismember a living human being in nature's protective womb, you are capable of any atrocity.

It has taken pounds of cocaine and other drugs to dull our collective consciousness to the point where national papers announce that 47% of Irish women have had abortions and where pro aborts claim that 67% of Irish residents support abortion.

Statistical sources are not clear: polls can easily be rigged. Government statistics are fairly reliable.

The majority of Irish citizens live abroad and are excluded from the right to vote and the right to express any opinion on issues relevant to Ireland. Hence the reference to "residents."

Transplants require lifetime use of anti-rejection and other medications. An infant gestated in a transplanted uterus will always be at risk.

Then again, we've accepted the practice of over-stimulating ovaries, fertilizing large numbers of ova, creating "supplies" of cryogenically warehoused babies in waiting.
When the woman or parents decide they're "ready" for their child, a number of embryo are injected into the womb, allowed to become viable.

They are then scanned, and the mother selects which of the little pre-nates will be killed by an injection of poison into his/her little heart. The mother...!

And fathers accompany their girl friends to the killing rooms.

75% of relationships break up following abortion.

Drive in the country side during nesting season and you'll wonder if the little birds are playing "banzai" or kamikaze as they dart out of the hedgerows into the path of an oncoming car.

These are avian fathers putting their lives on the line to protect their avian offspring.

The human male legislates to kill the human child - on behalf of women's rights.

New York City is one of the abortion capitals of the world. In eighties, the streets were barren of children. In the nineties there was a turnaround and now the streets are clogged with double strollers as multiple births dominate.

Multiple births dominate because abortion damages the female reproductive system, causing scarring of the fallopian tubes, damage to uterus or bladder: it increases the risk of ectopic pregnancy, infertility, miscarriage.

These problems can also occur spontaneously in nature.

I have treated Infertility homeopathically without intrusive or ignominious protocols with a 95% success rate.

We turn our minds from the horror of the removal of organs from living human beings in Chinese prisons. This to ensure "viability" or "freshness."

Beautiful, evocative words such as "harvest" and "freshness" now offer nauseating connotations. Language is becoming as polluted and toxic as the sky over China.

Speaking of words, how strange that the term "limbo" disappeared just as "frozen embryo" emerged.

Will the adult survivor of embryonic cryogenics have a latent fear of cold? Will he/she ever be able to enjoy an ice-cream?

A new internet crime has emerged: the seduction of innocents by webcrawlers who lure them into a "meeting" place, then render them unconscious before removing a kidney or two!

Women made pregnant through internet "romances," and are then persuaded to give up their child for "private adoption" should report threats or coercion to the police.

"Private adoption" can be a euphemism for baby trafficking.

The human pre-nate has become a commodity to be bartered.

If a baby can be dismembered, saltburned in utero, frozen as an embryo, discarded as unwanted or sliced up in a laboratory or used for body parts, what then can be precious or important in life?

Commodities?

In my homeopathic work I have proven the teachings of Homeopathy's founding fathers and mothers, incredibly brave physicians who tested the remedy on themselves, taking copious and infinite notes on seemingly innocuous symptoms. Said "peculiar" symptoms are now the prescribers "best friends."

My work, their work, and the work of thousands of Classical Homeopathists around the world prove that the cruel and inhuman experiments adopted by orthodox science are completely unnecessary. We have cured the "incurables," sometimes in difficult conditions where the patient's access to good nutrition, physiotherapy etc., was limited, or the patient discouraged from treatment by skeptical family members or colleagues.

There is really no need for fetal stem research.

It is a subject most people prefer not to dwell on, and so it continues, contributing a dangerous disthymic buzz to the collective unconscious of decent folk everywhere.

Where a child is lost via spontaneous abortion, anniversaries are distressing and should be marked with compassion and kindness. However, the suicidal factor is considerably diminished here.

CHAPTER EIGHTEEN

POST NATAL DEPRESSION

This is a heartbreak. Ideally, a mother's joy at holding her squeaking, squawky, sometimes screaming, spitting up child - the most beautiful one ever born by the way - over-rides all "local" problems such as hospital bills, squabbling grandmas, sibling rivalry, (it happens!) even absent fathers.

One look at "little squeaky" and the body floods with endorphins suffusing every pore with peace and joy and bliss and delight.

Given such expectations, a new mom might try to conceal her Post Natal Depression. (PND) She might feel ashamed, embarrassed, overwhelmed by the experience of childbirth. She may be in too much pain, or have sustained injury during the birth trauma. She may pretend to enjoy her baby, when in fact the prospect of caring for the child fills her with dread.

She may have come through an abandoned pregnancy alone, without the foot-rubs and indulgences of a protective and loving husband.

She may have had a wonderful husband, but the depression relates to past issues, hormonal imbalance, genetic susceptibility.

She may be suffering from PAS. The combination of PAS and PND are potentially lethal for children.

Especially within two years of giving birth.

An informal ad hoc study of women in prison for infanticide reveals a significant number with histories of abortion and the birth of a child within two years.

Untreated, the gestation of an infant provides an acutely painful reminder that the aborted baby was a human being. This can trigger a profound sense of loss or guilt which is then transferred to surviving children. The mother can feel that the children are better off in another place without her. Or she just loses the inability to cope.

Social/Market forces continue to promote abortion, ignoring its profoundly destructive effects on the female psyche.
Waking up to its effects on men, might turn attitudes around.

Spousal relations are usually reserved for forty days after birth, in order to allow the womb to heal, and give mommy a chance to recover. Sexual rejection is probably the first time Daddy realizes that all is not well, but signs and symptoms are evident to post natal carers. Professionals are trained to observe for PND.

The UK has an excellent system of Visiting Nurses and follow-up care for new moms. The US system is top heavy with ante-natal care, rules, regulations, mandatory procedures, shots, etc. Ante-natal care is first rate in the USA, but post natal care is practically non existent. The systemn abandons new mothers to their own devices, save for a six week check up of mother and child. (This is NYC experience. Other states may do better.)

It's one of the coldest, callous systems imaginable in a Western society. It is hardly surprising that infanticide is frequent, frightening and unaddressed.

The public medical system takes the basic "you are our property" attitude and piles on meanness, aggression, bullying.

These are extrinsic factors which must eventually be addressed for the sake of family and community mental health.

In the meantime, it is my opinion that past abuse of women in labor in New York hospitals contributed to a high mortality rate along with substandard housing for the poor and its own form of Mugabeism - institutional bullying of immigrant whites. This is diminishing, but there is still little care and concern for the new single mommy.

Post Natal Depression is a highly dangerous condition which puts a mother at risk of suicide and infanticide, especially when coupled with Post Abortion Syndrome. Fathers may also suffer from PND and a sense of

Chapter XVIII   127

displacement. They can feel resentful of the squeaky little thing that not only keeps him up at night, but has subsumed his wife's every waking moment.

This is where father can become the prince in the family or the best friend of the remote control and the living room couch.

For a couple of months, you may feel that you are at the mercy of two tyrants - mother and child. Patient, loving care at this time will pay dividends later. Your wife may seem enraptured by the little squaller, but she is highly aware of your presence, your attitude, your practical support, and when she's a little stronger and baby is past the critical stage and well on his way to becoming sportsman/woman of the year, your wife will show her appreciation and pride in her husband.

Don't "bottle" this one or try to be brave.
You have a natural right to enjoy and celebrate your baby.
If you don't, speak to someone trustworthy and "tuned in" As Soon As Possible.

Looking at your beautiful child with "fear and loathing" does not make you a monster.
Failing to get help can destroy your life and that of your baby.

Homeopaths have wonderful remedies for emotional alienation.
Counsellors are trained to understand your emotional needs.
Alternative medicines can be very soothing.
Orthodox medicine (GP/MD) has diagnostic tools to explore endocrinal or hormonal causes of your profound anhedonia. [27]

It's alright to cry.

That is an excellent emotional release.

The absence of tears would be a matter for concern and suggest emotional blockage.

[27] Anhedonia - inability to experience joy

Your baby loves and misses you.

If you can, take care of him/her as much as possible. Perform acts of bathing and nappy changing with soft music and scents that you enjoy. Put as much kindness as you can into the actions.

Do not expect overnight results.

Caring for the baby in such away, will release you from guilt trauma when the natural feelings find release.

They will also build trust between you and your child and help the baby feel less abandoned.

He/she will experience your emotional absence, so healthy allow family members playtime with the baby.

Let go of any feelings of jealousy because others enjoy your baby.

This is your baby. He/she will know when you are back.

With joy to you both.

CHAPTER NINETEEN

STRATEGIES FOR SURVIVAL

TALK, TALK, TALK!

Express your pain.

Find a friend or professional. Get it out of your system.

Write, draw, punch a pillow. Play music, pray. In mild cases, watch someone else's misery - watch a mope-soap opera.

It's OK to scream - let it out in a safe place. Don't frighten children. Or grandmothers.

Reward and treat yourself.

If something is making you angry, find ways of dealing with it. Don't bottle it. If it is out of your control, try to let it go.

Make sure you are not cheating yourself.

Where society is unjust, the search for justice can be frustrating.

For instance, firing from a job for a specious reason, followed by the discovery that your replacement is the boss's best friend's niece.

In a just society you have redress through labour boards, civil action, etc.

Irish justice has developed from a closed, feudal, nepotistic, post-colonial state. It is now borrowing heavily, not from the best of the US, with its Constitutional Freedoms, but from Americas war lock-down and, understandable, anti-terror paranoia.

It appears that European leaders have been chowing down for Thanksgiving

Dinner at Quantico, as so many returned with Orwellian concepts. Who wants to challenge those at Christmas? Who has time?

Ireland now has a Garda auxiliary, comprised of civilians. It worked for Nazi Germany, The Soviet Union, Pinochet, etc.

Why not Ireland?

Because the people do not speak up. The people are uninformed. The people are invested in powerlessness.

Powerlessness leads to hopelessness, leads to suicide.

Speaking up can be risky. Politically, socially and within the family.

Starting small, a family may be invested in keeping a lid on secrets, and blow off your concerns defensively or derisively.

They may just button up. They may try to make you feel bad about yourself.

That's not your fault, unless you allow it.

No one can make you feel less about yourself without your permission.

You do not have to accept a stranger's opinion of you. Nor a family member's.

KNOW YOURSELF.

YOUR STRENGTHS, YOUR WEAKNESSES.

Work on your weaknesses. **Develop your talents and gifts.**
Remember you are allowed to profit from your gifts.
Scripture says so. Society respects you better when you respect yourself.

Expression defeats depression.

OCCULTISM

I do not recommend any participation in necromancy.

The better the psychic, the faster I flee.

Carl Jung treated certain cards as functions of the unconscious mind.

I accepted that explanation, but now believe that he was mistaken.

Some of my patients, desperately in need of love and affection, took to calling the psychic lines, and became increasingly addicted and indebted to these services.

If depression or suicidal ideation follows participation in activities traditionally tabooed by Judeo Christian societies, immediately consult a priest, clergyman or rabbi.

If they are secularist in outlook, ie, dismiss fears of the occult as nonsense look elsewhere.

Expect a reasonable inquiry to determine if your fears are related to generalized anxiety or if there is validity to any supernatural activity.

I expect studies to show a higher than average incidence of violent death in persons heavily involved in occultism.

These are perilous times for our youth. They are bombarded with psycho-sexual sadism, violence, occultism every time they turn on the TV, go to the movies, or open a game 'app.'

The character images are domineering, aggressive and, frankly, hideous.
Story lines are belligerent, war centered and supernatural.

Dungeon and Dragons, Harry Potter, etc., are all so innocent sounding. After all, the story of King Arthur had a magician -Merlin- and a witch - Morgana le fee.

Difference being that up to the seventies, children had a wealth and variety of stories, characters, both faith based and secular, and a strong grounding in a Judeo Christian Faith centered on the Mosaic Ten Commandments and a relationship with God.

Now occultism has become mainstream, and, again, bombarded at our children and teens, giving them a false sense of power, and of the warped values of using any amoral, immoral or violent strategies to attain their personal goals.

Now, ever seen a friend consult a 'psychic' or 'fortune teller' and be impressed at the personal knowledge this person has on him/her? Sometimes it's just a clever con artist at work, but other times it's darker and more dangerous. The 'psychic' has opened his or herself to the occult world, which is intrinsically destructive and will claim a bitter price. Your highly impressed friend will keep on returning, but the sharp, acute 'readings' no longer come through, and in the meantime, your friend has forgotten how to think for her/himself and becomes increasingly dependent on 'Madame X's Murky Readings.' His/Her life starts to become unmanageable, and falls apart, putting him/her at risk for suicide.

START OVER! Baby steps at first, but move toward the LIGHT!

CHAPTER TWENTY

DEPRESSION'S MASK AND MIRRORS

Depression is repressed pain.
Depression is anger buried deep within a human person.
Depression is a biochemical vortex.
Depression may be a symptom of physical disease.
Depression may be inherited or socialized.
Depression is the opposite of expression.

Masks and mirrors: Depression can take different forms and disguises:

<u>Vegetative</u>, where the sufferer tends to withdraw, lose appetite, avoid socialization.

<u>Agitated</u>, with restlessness, monologies, ie, talking without listening for a response. Talking masks communication, blocks emotional contact. It is a form of escape.

Restlessness of depression is unfocused and unproductive. Creative people often precede an intense project by a period of restlessness or fidgeting. Baffling as this may be to more settled personalities, ensuing productivity marks the difference between depression and healthy creativity.

Tangential note: The tendency to label creative people as schizophrenics or Aspergers or autistic is absurd. Artists (generic here for musicians, inventors, fine artists, writers, etc) are gifted, sensitive people, sacrificing a great deal to share their vision of beauty with the world. They are often exploited, discouraged and malnourished. Van Gogh is iconic in the "schizoid artists" world: this was a man whose brother warehoused his work in order to profit from it after Van Gogh's demise. He lived on wine and black coffee with the occasional bean soup and worked frenetically, wondering why no one bought his work. Mozart wrote over a thousand works of music. He only heard 300 of those works. In other words, 700 rejection slips. He continued to write, unpaid. How mad.

Where women are concerned, for every Bronte, Jane Austin or Beatrix Potter who achieved some success during their lifetime, how many, like Emily Dickinson, had to die before their work is acknowledged.

If it is an illness to continue to work despite poverty and disillusionment, then indeed most artists are sick. But if expression is an ultimate sign of good mental health, and altruism, self-sacrifice and sharing, are also indicators of good mental health, then we must continue to respect and uphold the genuinely gifted.

After all, they make fortunes for collectors and keep academics in payslips.

Usually less critical than vegetative, agitated depression can be a dangerous symptom, especially when the restlessness is stepped up and when accompanied by suicidal actions or expression.

This can be effectively treated with Homeopathic protocols, [28] but the patient, whenever possible, must be permitted choice of treatment.

Restraints should only be used in extremis. They are cruel, undignified and exacerbate the patient's sense of powerlessness. They can also induce cardiac arrest.

Ice baths and ECTs testify to the poverty of orthodox medicine in the understanding and treatment of mental illness.

<u>*Disthymic depression*</u> *is marked by functionality but where the patient is aware of something missing and feels a general sense of discontent. Life is pleasant enough, but he/she becomes aware of a general inability to feel pleasure. They project their discontent via lethargy, or pessimism. They become passive-aggressive, finding subtle ways to project their unhappiness on others. It is*

---

[28] *"Nothing convinced me of the efficacy of Homeopathic medicine more than its use in the case of a woman determined to commit suicide. In a short space of time she attempted to defenestrate, cut herself and place her head into a gas oven. The administration of a single dose of the (appropriate remedy) calmed her, eased her restlessness..." This is a paraphrase. The direct quotes are in my notes in a packing case in NYC. I don't identify the remedy as it would tempt the uninformed to use it in every case of attempted suicide. An experienced Homeopathist can identify this from the foregoing quote.*

often rooted in powerlessness; for example, where a child has had to assume adult responsibilities, never experiencing the freedom and crazy joys of being a child, and who grows into a world of similar relentless obligations.

On the surface all is normal. However, ultimately, social alienation is inevitable, and, untreated, the disthymic depressive becomes vegetative and progressive.
A good medical work-up is immensely valuable in diagnosing underlying physiological causes of disthymic depression.

<u>*Psychotic Depression*</u> *is marked by delusional expressions, hallucination or manifestations of persecution.*

Such expressions should not be automacally dismissed.

In NYC, many Irish women were subject to racist abuse. The Octagon building on Roosevelt Island, source of much disgust to one Charles Dickens, housed Irish immigrant women driven to nervous breakdowns by harsh working conditions.

As domestics, they were on call round the clock. If subjected to sexual harassment, they were summarily dismissed. If raped on the job with ensuing pregnancy, the East River was a few blocks away.

Fast forwarding to the turn of the Millennium, and another dynamic emerges. In the rush to educate as many minorities as possible, the Irish were somehow overlooked.

In fact, the Irish are now the 7% minority in NYC, but receive no special privileges or assistance. Irish immigrant women and Irish American women managed to achieve supervisory positions without the benefit of a college education. In business and in hospitals, the Irish were valued by bosses, but harassed and bullied by so called minorities until driven out of employment and into nervous breakdowns.

I know those women. I have met and spoken with them. They are *fantastic* women, innately strong, kind, generous. They took care of their siblings. They sent money back home. They endured long hours, low pay and insensitive employers to provide for their families while the father stayed home on the land.

In every other culture, the father left, sending home money for his family. In Ireland, many fathers left and did provide for their families. Others succumbed to the depression of life as tenth rate immigrant in the UK and abandoned their children for booze. It was that or suicide in the damp, hungry tenements. Misery on both side of the Irish sea.

Individual priests worked heroically among these communities, but the official attitude in Ireland was one of officious contempt. The Church in Ireland was more ceremonial than pastoral. Elements of this continue to the present, and, combined with the fall out of the Church-State pedophile cover-ups, have left the faithful with a profound sense of betrayal and mistrust.

"To whom, Lord, shall we go?"

GK Chesterton wrote that when a man lost his Faith, he didn't just believe in *anything*: he believed *everything*.

CHAPTER TWENTY-ONE

WHEN BEREAVED BY SUICIDE

Bereavement and loss are painful enough. Survivors do not need the additional burden of guilt.

"Should have, could have, would have…" have no place in the grieving room.

A suicide may be surrounded by a loving, supportive family and still be unable to cope. Sadly, that love and support may make sharing a burden or experience of guilt or shame more difficult.

Self inflicted death is violent, painful, and brutal on survivors.

Do not make worse on yourself by taking responsibility for the actions of another.

Do not torture yourself with "what ifs?"

A suicide can be very calculated. If you *did* make the call you regret not making you can then torture yourself with something said or unsaid.

Given the human body's economy, its innate and atavistic drive to life, and the neurological processes of dying, there must always come a moment of regret, an opportunity of repentance.

That regret and repentance may open the door of Heaven to the suicide.

But it's best not to judge.

Celebrate the decease, his/her life and gifts.

Light a candle and talk to him/her. Tell him/her how angry you feel, how sad you feel, how much you miss him/her. If you are a Catholic, have Mass offerings. If another faith, remember him/her at prayer meetings.

Do an act of kindness in his/her name.

Acknowledge your grief and be kind to yourself.

Your loved one would want that.

Remember you a rare and precious person:

You are the only one of you in the entire world.

Your relationship with the deceased does not end with death. It continues. If you feel that the spirit of your deceased beloved is still troubled, speak lovingly to him/her. Express your anger or loneliness. Light a candle and have a quiet moment together. If you feel anger or fear, offer prayers or a Mass. Keep this up until peace "comes dropping slow, dropping like the veil of Heaven upon the earth below…" It may take years to free your beloved from whatever bound, or hurt him/her to breaking point, but the peace will come.

Do not invoke séances or psychics. That is only inviting trouble into your home or mind.

POST BEREAVEMENT

Loss of a beloved family member or friend can trigger strange and uncomfortable emotions. [29]

It may be frightening to experience a desire to join the missing beloved, too frightening to share with other family members.

It's important to seek counseling. The "copycat" ideation can be compelling.

Loss may be experienced as anger, abandonment, anhedonia, [30] abandon-

[29]
[30] Inability to experience joy

ment, depression, irritability, tearfulness, sadness, dissociation, even sadness.

Sleeplessness is common and quite dangerous. A tired mind cannot defend itself. Develop strategies for coping with that. Herbal teas, soft music: the BBC news and Discovery channels have been mentioned on more than one occasion by patients as helpful to insomnia.

Emotions cover the extreme sorrow of permanent loss, of knowing that you will never see, hear, touch or hold a beloved friend or family member. The loss of a pet cannot be underestimated.

Our angels fly to Heaven because they take themselves lightly!
G.K. Chesterton

http://angelsandsaintsandus.blogspot.com/2013/07/padre-pio-guardian-angels-and-miracle.html
www.padrepio.catholicwebservices.com/ENGLISH/Guard.htm

CHAPTER TWENTY TWO

COPING WITH THE ULTIMATE TRAGEDY

My friend found his brother hanging in the garden. He was a gentle man, single, orderly, professional, chronically depressed and medicated. Classic story of a psychologist who helped everyone but himself.

My friend is a priest. He established that there was no hope of resuscitation, and anointed his brother's body. He had to leave it for the police to find.

He said that if he had done nothing else in his life, anointing his brother was the one thing that made it worthwhile.

He sent his other brother to prevent their mother from looking out the window and prayed by the body till the police and ambulance arrived and cut his brother down.

I hadn't seen "Fr. X" for almost a year but knew immediately that something had happened.

There was a shock and pain in his eyes even after months of bereavement counseling.

It was important for him to speak about his brother, to remember the loving and generous man; to express sorrow for his pain and sadness for his mother. We spoke of God's way of bringing good out of evil.

X has grown and matured through this.

He spoke with sadness and regret that he could not help his brother, who was on medication at the time of his death.

He also spoke with grace and serenity. He accepted that he was powerless to change his brother's intention.

Despite his own physical frailties, Fr. X is committed in his service to humanity. His brother's suicide strengthened that commitment.

"C" terminated his own life on Mother's Day. His sister found him hanging.

He must have been very angry with his mother, "Jane" a feisty gal from Northern Ireland who had emigrated to the USA with a drunk, abusive husband who negative her musical gifts and encouraged her to support his career by becoming a nurse and working all hours.

He died after their divorce and "C" seems to have blamed his mother. He turned to drugs and eventually took his own life.

Choosing Mother's Day was particularly cruel and unusual punishment for his mother. The approach to Mother's Day filled "Jane" with anguish; her moods changed, she lashed out at people, and was too ashamed to say why.

I'm not a big drinker, but I joined her in a Bushmills that she had brought back from Belfast, where she had lost a sister and a brother to old age and infirmity.

She started to speak about "C." She was defensive, feared judgment, condemnation.

I listened, let her affirm "C" but knew that healing would take some time. She was ripped apart with grief, loss, anger. The choice of Mother's Day seemed almost spiteful; on the other hand, it may have given the poor man the consolation that he would never be forgotten.

For the next couple of years I watched out for her around Mother's Day, making a point to invite her for tea or lunch, never mentioning her son, unless she brought him up. And she usually did.

One day when I returned from a visit to Ireland, she invited me in for tea, and said that she was at peace with her son, that she felt his presence very strongly and that they had forgiven one another.

She died that year. At peace with herself and her son.

Chapter XXII

Here I would like to apologise to a little girl named Cheryl. We are both adults now and I have no idea where she is, but she lived close to our house in England when I was four years old.

My mother was raised by very superstitious servants in South America. When she heard that Cheryl's mother had committed suicide she told us not to speak to Cheryl.

That poor child eventually asked myself and my older sister why we wouldn't play with her.

I told her that we were very sorry, but we were not allowed to, and gave her the reason why.

That was more than thirty years ago. To this day I remember the stricken, hurt look in her eyes.

Needless to say, her poor Dad paid my parents a visit that night, but the damage was done.

They moved away, but I have never forgotten Cheryl and her large, shocked eyes.

I wish I could turn the clock back and hug her.

Such cruelties should not occur in the Third Millennium. Persons bereaved by suicide should receive all the love and support that we can give them. Children, in particular, must never experience abandonment and rejection from the living persons supporting them.

Even the death of a favorite entertainer or childhood role model can trigger depression and a sense that life is moving on without you. Death represents loss and change.

- *Take time to grieve.*
- *Accept that this is one thing you cannot change, that death is irreversible.*
- *Take time to celebrate the good experiences, the personal qualities, the intimacies of a friendship/relationship.*

- *Speak to your deceased friend. Even pagan faiths recognize the spiritual connection between ancestors and loved ones. The relationship does not end with the death of the body. Avoid necromancers and séances. They have the potential to bring in uninvited, destructive forces.*
- *Catholics have developed a theology of the Communion of Saints which acknowledges the continuing relationship of persons of faith both sides of "the curtain" and in ultimate reunion. Other faiths believe in life after death.*

- *Allow yourself to grieve in your own time, your own style.*

- *Privately or with a friend, a good cup of tea, a light drink.*

- *Members of a bereavement group will have shared the stages that you are going through; these include anger, denial, shock, sadness, acceptance, resolution. In different orders.*

- *Avoid binge drinking or drugging.*

- *Do not blame yourself for "words" or arguments that may have occurred prior to the suicide.*

- *Arguments and conflicts most likely grew out of concern for the loved one. Some suicides act very calmly and "normally" while planning to end their lives, but most do give off signals; cris du coeur, [31] questionable remarks about death or accidents, unusual drinking or social conduct.*

The loss of a beloved is an experience of abandonment. The deceased has not chosen to abandon you, but that does not alter the profound sense of loss.

The love that existed before bereavement never dies.

It blesses the universe forever.

CHAPTER TWENTY THREE

MORE ON STRATEGIES

Again:

- **Talk, talk, talk.**

- **Bite the bullet** - *toughing it out alone may work for some, but "bottling" usually increases the internal pressure and pain of depression. Don't feel you have to do it alone.*

- **Avoid mood altering substances** - you often feel worse when the anaesthetic effects wear off. Alcohol, for example, is a depressive.

- **Avoid toxic friends.**
These are people who leave you feeling worse rather than better. They are emotional bullies who transfer their own rage onto others and derive perverse satisfaction from the control and subsequent suffering of others.

*Depression, being a complex disease, can lead its victim to seek destructive experiences and toxic friends. For example, the abused wife who determines to leave the abuser but **sabotages her decision** by finding a religious formalist to convince her that faith obliges her to remain with a violent sadist.*

A gentle man, depressed by bullying at work, or the lack of promotion, gets up the courage to find a new job, but "bumps into" the one "buddy" with jealousy or other issues who convinces him to stay in a soul destroying environment.

A women who puts herself in danger by habituating dicey nightclubs, or taking strangers home; a man who takes uncalculated risks, eg, driving drunk, etc., are all manifesting symptoms of profound depression and call for professional help. They can be a heartbreaking, bottomless pit for an untrained buddy.

By definition, a friend is supportive and nurturing. He/she may not have all the answers, or professional knowledge, but is willing to listen and make suggestions, or just listen. Genuine concern and openness are priceless, and sometimes a few kind words and warm smile are enough to unlock the door to recovery...

Caveat: Kindness may be initially met by bitterness, but it is a powerful seed and usually takes root. If not there is a comfort in knowing that, at least, one tried.

- **It's OK to scream**, just not in the presence of children.
  Unaddressed pain can become like a pressure cooker, building and building. It's OK to scream, but **it's better to take a long, rapid walk**. This will oxygenate the brain, and work off destructive epeniphrenes. (eg, adrenalin)

- **Get it out of your system**. It's better to talk, to write, to paint, to communicate, to *express pain* than to hold it in.
  Japanese corporations are renowned for innovative employee relations. They provide rooms where an employee can release anger and frustration. American corporations may provide counselors, who, however, keep detailed notes and records, offshoots of a litigious culture. Where professional survival is based on a culture of smiling and kissing up to the boss, it is better to keep personal communication and self-expression outside the work place and privately devise rewards and strategies for coping in a difficult environment.

"Julie" was a corporate executive, used to the company helicopters, and a sophisticated life. Returning home she saw a man leap from the roof of her building, followed by men in suits and dark glasses. She was completely traumatized and came to my office, where providence had provided a cancellation and long lunch hour. She stayed for a couple of hours, and was somewhat improved by the time she left, but the nightmares continued and she took a vacation. She said that she started swimming in the Caribbean, swimming too far out to sea, when suddenly five dolphins appeared and started playing with her.

At that point she felt extraordinary peace and delight. She said hours elapsed, without her realizing it, and as the sun set, the dolphins pushed her into the shore. From that day, she felt "normal" again, or better than, because she started to believe in a Higher Power.

The creatures of God carry His healing graces.

"A mother may leave her child but I will not abandon you" says the Lord...

Do you believe that you are powerless?

We all have power - to stay, to leave, to change, and do face down our enemies.

Even if they appear to be twice our size!

CHAPTER TWENTY FOUR

Postlude: For Persons of Faith

For persons of faith, fear of eternal damnation of a loved one may shadow their lives. Where faith becomes a burden rather than a blessing, the precepts of that Faith must be re-examined with a compassionate clergy or person of deep Faith.

Christians believe in the infinite Mercy of God. All knowing, all seeing, omnipresent, He alone truly understands and heals the disordered soul. He alone has the right of judgment, which is not the materialistic, power oriented judgment of humankind.

Let go. Let God.

Read the psalms quietly. Listen to the response.

Light a candle and speak with your loved one.

Light a candle and listen to your loved one.

> **Faith moves mountains.**
> **Faith as minute as a mustard seed can transform the world.**
> **Faith unifies Heaven and Earth.**
> **Faith is Faith, an extraordinary gift.**
> **It comes with angels**
> **Angels come with supernatural powers, of comfort and joy. Of protection, healing and communication.**
> **They are a whisper away.**

Every soul has been endowed with an extraordinary protector called an angel. Despite mass marketing and media attempts to trivialize their image the power and miraculous intervention of angels continues to be witnessed and recorded. Awesome!

Tell your Guardian Angel how you are feeling. That you feel sad and hopeless, dangerously so. Ask your Guardian Angel to help you, and hold on for the response. It may not be quite how you expect it. God speaks more often in whispers than in the voice of thunder but He never fails to respond.

Your Guardian Angel can communicate with the Angel of your beloved. You may humbly ask your angel to send a message of love and consolation to the angel of your loved one.

Be very respectful to your invisible protectors and ask humbly for protection. These are awesome spirits. Terrifying if they were unaccompanied by love.

But they are an expression of God's love for us, and the sooner we all start listening, the better.

Listening and understanding takes practice and prayer.

It does not happen overnight - except in emergencies.

It's hard to hear when the mind is full of clutter and fear and anxiety and porn and drugs or alcohol.

Warnings are ignored or lost.

Time spent in daily prayer is its own reward.

Time spent in daily prayer or meditation brings many rewards.

If you are in too much pain to speak, light a candle; let that light shine in God's presence on your behalf.

On behalf of your loved one.

Believe and you shall see.

The bereaved often assume an unnecessary guilt. Bring that to an understanding priest in confession. If he's not understanding, leave politely and find one who is. The other may be dealing with issues that affect his ability to relate with compassion.

Chapter XXIV

If you are not Catholic, speak with a member of your clergy. If your Faith is judgmental and harsh to suicides, then speak to a secular counselor. You do not need any more grief or "shame-blame" projections.

The 23rd Psalm is probably the best known of the psalms. Around the world, it is the psalm of choice for Christian funerals.

Judeo Christian theology is condensed into a few eloquent lines.

> *The Lord is my Shepherd*
> *I shall not want...*

It is seldom read or discussed in the context of the preceding Psalm, which is a pity. Taken together they form a dialogue.

In Psalm 22, the psalmist is filled with despair and begs for help.

I hear Psalm 23 as a direct response from a loving Father, and put it in the first person:

> **I, the Lord,** *am your Shepherd*
> You shall not want
> **I, the Lord,** will bring to green pastures
> Where you will find repose
>
> **I, the Lord,** will anoint your head with oil
> In the presence of your foes
> **I, the Lord,** will anoint your head with oil
> And fill your cup to overflowing.

Given history's tendency to stone people who claim direct dialogue with God, I wonder if the psalmist adjusted the text.

Comfort ye my people.

Thus says the Lord. [32]

Deepest gratitude to all friends and spiritual advisers who supported and encouraged me through the writing of this book.

Because of the sensitivity of the subject names are presently withheld from publication.

In a particular way I would like to dedicate this work to the woman who inspired it, a reader of Irish Catholic who directed me to the need for some insights on the subject. A complimentary copy will be set aside for her.

---

[1] Isaiah - "The Messiah"

CPSIA information can be obtained
at www.ICGtesting.com
Printed in the USA
LVHW082133040919
629995LV00009B/700/P